Together *for* Festivals

Resources for All-age Worship

Together *for* Festivals

Resources for All-age Worship

Edited by Pam Macnaughton and Hamish Bruce

Illustrations by Simon Smith

NATIONAL SOCIETY/CHURCH HOUSE PUBLISHING

CHURCH HOUSE, GREAT SMITH STREET, LONDON SW1P 3NZ

Church House Publishing
Church House
Great Smith Street
London SW1P 3NZ

ISBN 0 7151 4893 1

Published in 1997 by The National Society and Church House Publishing

Compilation © *The National Society 1997*

Illustrations © *Simon Smith*

Acknowledgements

The editors and publisher gratefully acknowledge permission to use copyright material in this publication. Every effort has been made to trace and contact copyright holders. If there are any inadvertent omissions we apologize to those concerned.

Extracts from *The Alternative Service Book 1980* (p. 91) and *Patterns for Worship* (Church House Publishing, 1995) (p. 89) are copyright © The Central Board of Finance of the Church of England and are reproduced by permission.

Extract (pp. 90–91) from Michael Perry (ed.), *Church Family Worship* (Hodder & Stoughton, 1987) is copyright © Mrs B. Perry / Jubilate Hymns Ltd and is reproduced by permission.

Extract (p. 125) from Peter Graystone and Eileen Turner, *A Church for All Ages* (Scripture Union, 1993) is copyright © Peter Graystone and Eileen Turner and is reproduced by permission of the publisher.

Cover design by Julian Smith

Printed in England by Biddles Ltd, Guildford and King's Lynn

Contents

Harvest 107

All Saints/Saints 121

Introduction

Colour, excitement, anticipation, discovery, repentance, celebrations, parties, new faith – the list of elements that make up the festivals of the Church's year could go on and on. They are occasions to make the most of, times of wonder to cherish, and opportunities for exploring new depths of revealed truth. Certainly those whose responsibility it is to plan the worship and activities for these treasured times of year may hope for all these.

In reality it is often a struggle to make the well-worn stories fresh and captivating to hearers. Somehow, people who are new to it all – whether because they are children growing into understanding, or new attenders at church – need to be catered for, as well as those who have heard the stories countless times before. We need to be searching constantly for creative ways of saying it all.

We are therefore very pleased to offer this anthology. Such collections have proved very popular in the past. Two-thirds of this book is made up of material for festivals from *Together with Children* magazine over the last couple of years. The other third is previously unpublished material. The pieces can be adapted to fit your own situation, and we are confident that you will find suggestions here to help you plan lively celebrations, or at the very least to spark off new ideas.

Pam Macnaughton
Editor, *Together with Children* magazine.

List of Abbreviations

EH — *The English Hymnal*, Oxford University Press, 1933

HAMNS — *Hymns Ancient and Modern New Standard*, Hymns Ancient and Modern Limited, 1983

HAMR — *Hymns Ancient and Modern Revised*, The Canterbury Press Norwich, 1996

HON — *Hymns Old and New,* New Anglican Edition, Kevin Mayhew, 1996

JP — *Junior Praise*, Marshall Pickering, 1986

MP — *Mission Praise*, Marshall Pickering

SF — *Songs of Fellowship*, Kingsway Music, 1991

WP — *World Praise*, Marshall Pickering, 1995

Advent and Christmas

Advent craft activities

JOHN 8:12 Jesus said "I am the Light of the World"

Advent is a time of preparation, anticipation and waiting as we look forward to the coming of Jesus into the world. We can help the children to mark the days and weeks in Advent by having one or more of the following at church, in our groups, and in their homes.

Advent wreath

An Advent wreath is an arrangement of greenery (holly, ivy, laurel, etc.) with four red or purple candles set into it. One of these is lit on the first Sunday in Advent, two on the second and so on, until on the fourth Sunday all are lit. In the centre there is a larger white candle which is only lit on Christmas Day. Against this candle can be rested a card showing the words from John's Gospel (8.12) when Jesus said, 'I am the light of the world. The person who follows me will never live in darkness, but he will have the light that gives life.'

Children can be involved in collecting the greenery and making the Advent wreath for use in the church and in their groups. A poster-type picture of an Advent wreath can be made by the children for their homes. A black background is good. Leaves cut out of different types of green paper can make the wreath. Red candles can be cut from vibrant red paper or foil. A foil flame can be stuck on the candle to be 'lit' each week. A large white candle can be stuck on for Christmas Day with a caption giving the words of John 8.12. This can stay in the children's homes throughout Advent and Christmas.

The building of the Advent wreath over the four-week period helps a child to experience the sense of anticipation. There are some songs available to use at the time of the candle-lighting ceremony.

Advent candles

Advent candles are readily available in the shops. A section of the candle is burned each day, showing children that Christmas is approaching.

If Advent candles are given to children to use each day in their homes, they should always be issued with appropriate precautionary notes about safety. Parents should be given these warn-

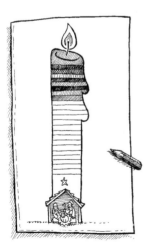

ings too. It is a good idea to suggest that the candle is burned at the family meal each day.

Because of the fire risk when using candles, much can be achieved with young children by making 'candles' from paper and card.

• *Candle drawings*

Draw a large candle on a sheet of paper. This can be either on A4 or A3-size paper for each child, and on a very much larger scale for a wall display in church or a community room. Divide the candle into 24 sections. Have a nativity scene at the foot of the candle. Each day the appropriate section of the candle is coloured in. The main nativity scene is coloured in at Christmas.

- *A 3-D model*

Collect 25 cardboard tubes of differing heights and thicknesses for each child (kitchen rolls, gift-wrapping rolls, etc.). Cut into different heights. Roll each tube with coloured paper so that each child has a collection of tubes of different colours and sizes.

Pack the inside of the tube with screwed-up newspaper, so that when the tube is glued onto its base board it is attached by a solid base and not just the rim of the tube. Number the tubes 1-25, ensuring that number 25 is the biggest candle and white/silver in colour. Cover a piece of strong cardboard with coloured paper, and stick the tubes to it in an attractive design. Stuff the tops of the candles with coloured tissue paper. Each child is given a box or tub (cottage-cheese pot with a lid) containing 25 flames. Each day the child 'lights' one of the candles by attaching a flame. The 3-D design can be decorated with spray-on snow, cotton wool, tinsel and glitter. Captions can be added, such as: 'It is nearly Jesus' birthday'.

I am counting the days to Jesus' birthday.

- *Candle poster*

If preferred, children can be given a blank sheet of coloured paper with a caption like: 'I am counting the days to Jesus' birthday'. They make, and keep in an envelope or box, 25 paper candles. Each day another candle is stuck onto the sheet and numbered.

- *Star poster*

A similar poster can be created by children who have a box containing 24 small and 1 large star. The backing sheet can carry a caption on it. Each day a child sticks a numbered star onto the backing sheet. When the large star is put onto the poster on Christmas Day it carries the wording: 'Happy Birthday Jesus. A star told of Jesus' birth'.

I am counting the days to Jesus' birthday

3

Making Advent calendars

It is easier to make large Advent calendars than small ones, because of the intricacy and time-consuming nature of cutting out a lot of small doors. On a large scale (such as a calendar the size of a display board), doors can be cut out on a hinge (i.e. cutting around three sides of a rectangle and leaving the fourth side attached to the backing sheet). The doors can be fastened down with mapping pins and made to look like door knobs – but ensure these are out of the reach of small children. The pictures behind the doors can be provided from carefully chosen Christmas cards. Neatly written texts can be added and games and activities made from learning these different verses of Scripture.

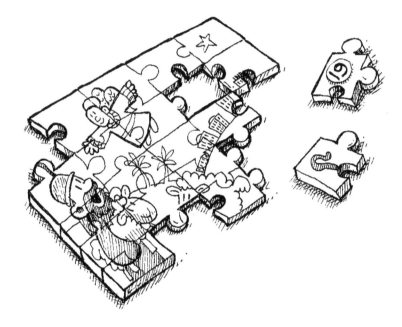

• *Colour-in Advent*

As an alternative, a picture can be divided into 25 pieces, like a jigsaw. Each section can be numbered and children are then invited to colour in the appropriate section each day. The picture is gradually completed as Christmas approaches.

• *Advent drawers*

Collect 25 boxes of the same size. Matchboxes are ideal but larger boxes can also be used. Cover the boxes with coloured paper, but ensure that they still open like a drawer. Stick them together to look like a chest of drawers. Mapping pins can also be used to aid opening. Stick the pin into the end of the box, and then attach a small knob of Blu-tack on the inside of the drawer, where the pin sticks through. This

prevents people from scratching themselves on the pin, and it prevents the 'door knob' from being pulled out. Number the drawers. If a large box of an appropriate size can be found for Christmas Day (day 25) then that would be especially appropriate. In each box there can be a tiny scroll bearing a verse of Scripture relating to the anticipation of the coming of Jesus, a sticker, a small picture cut off a card, etc. Each day the drawer is opened and its contents stuck on an Advent poster.

© Betty Pedley

Dress rehearsal

This is an Advent play for performance in church or school. It is suitable for children aged from about nine years to early teens. No scenery is required but there should be a door or screen to represent 'offstage'.

Cast

Teacher, Boy, Naomi and at least six other non-speaking boys and girls
(i.e. two angels, two shepherds, Joseph and Mary)

When the play begins the teacher is alone, holding a large box of props and costumes. The rest of the cast are amongst the audience.

Teacher (*To the audience*) I'm sorry to interrupt the service/class/assembly, but I'm afraid this is the last chance we have to rehearse for the nativity play. It should only take a few minutes. I hope you don't mind.

(*To the cast*) Now, would all the children who are in the play come to the front? I'll give you your costumes, then you can slip quietly through to the hall and we'll get on as quickly as we can.

Children (*Start moving forward, grumbling*) Dress rehearsal. Boring!

Teacher Here you are, Naomi, angel's wings for you. And you're a shepherd, aren't you, Jamie? (*Teacher ad libs as she hands things out. (Teacher ad libs as she hands things out. Children fool around . . . . 'I can fly, I can fly!) Children fool around – e.g. angel flaps her 'wings' and chants, 'I can fly, I can fly!'*)

Now stop making such a din and take your things into the hall QUIETLY! (*She herds the children out, then hesitates at the last moment.*)

Oh dear, we've forgotten Jesus. Naomi, pop back and see if Jesus is in the box, will you? (*Teacher exits and Naomi enters. Boy strolls onto the stage holding a broom. He starts picking up paper bags and putting them in the box.*)

Naomi Hello, are you new here?

Boy No, I've been around quite a while.

Naomi That's funny. I haven't seen you before. Why aren't you in the nativity play with the rest of us?

Boy I don't know. There didn't seem to be a part for me. I thought there might be some rubbish for me to clear up, though. There usually is.

Naomi That's nice.

Teacher (*Offstage*) Naomi?

Naomi (*Explaining to the boy*) We forgot Jesus, and she sent me to look for him. (*She rummages in the large box, and lifts out a baby doll.*) Here he is! Well, sorry you didn't get a part in the nativity play. Better luck next time.

Boy Yes, there's always Easter. In fact I know I've got the main part in that.

Naomi Great! I'll be seeing you again, then.

Boy I hope so. (*Naomi exits.*) Oh, I do hope so.

(*He carries a box of rubbish to the back of church. Children return to their seats in silence.*)

© Margaret Spivey

The girl who saw Christmas

This story, and its companion, The boy who saw Easter *are ideal as 'read aloud' stories to groups of primary-aged children.*

Miriam was in trouble again. She had knocked the earthenware lamp off its pedestal when she had hurriedly stumbled out of the small house to feed the donkey. 'You are such a scatter-brain!' cried her mother. 'Forgetting to feed him. I'll have to buy another lamp at the market in Bethlehem tomorrow. With the place crowded with strangers for the census it won't be easy getting about.'

Miriam knew what the census was. It was a head-count of all the families in Palestine ordered by the Roman Emperor Caesar Augustus whose soldiers occupied their country. Each male head of family had to go back to the town of his birth to be registered. Strangers had been arriving in the town for some weeks and then departing again after registering at the tax office. The inns had been doing good business and shopkeepers had made money out of this.

'I'm sorry' whispered ten-year-old Miriam.

'Off you go then and don't be long. I'll clear up.'

Her mother's voice was gentler as Miriam limped outside to the open shed. She had been born with her left leg slightly shorter than her right one, which often made her clumsy. She carried the bundle of hay in her arms. Animal feed was kept indoors in the winter out of the wind and the rain. As she watched the donkey nibbling, she remembered the man with his wife who had stopped to speak with her as she milked the goats that morning in the nearby pasture. The earthenware basin had been full of the creamy liquid from which her mother would make cheese for her father's lunch. He was a shepherd out on the hills with his flock, helped by her elder brother James, who was thirteen and now a man.

The lady had been beautiful sitting on the donkey with a warm cloak wrapped about her. A few tendrils of dark hair, escaping from her veil, were blowing in the wind. She smiled tenderly at Miriam from soft eyes. She was expecting a baby. Miriam knew. Her younger brother Peter had arrived a month before and her mother had looked like that before he was born, plump and tired. The lady's husband was older with a brown, lined face and dark beard under his turban.

'Little girl,' he had asked. 'Is it much further to Bethlehem? My wife is weary and I wish her to rest.'

'It's not far. You will see the town wall when you pass the next olive tree. And there are plenty of inns to stay at. Though they will be getting full now it's midday.'

She had stood up to point out the way. The man had listened patiently. He hadn't noticed her leg as some did, asking questions about it that she couldn't answer.

'Thank you, my dear,' he said and started to walk on.

'Wait!'

She loped indoors and fetched a beaker. Filling it with the warm and fragrant milk she handed it to the lovely lady to drink. She took it gratefully, thanking her in a soft musical voice. Afterwards, Miriam gave milk to her husband. The donkey was not forgotten. She let him sup noisily at the small water-trough that the goats used.

'May the Lord give you the desire of your heart, my child,' smiled the stranger and led the donkey down the hill, his wife swaying gently on the beast's back.

But Miriam had prayed to the Lord God before for the desire of her heart and he had not granted it.

Night fell. The stars shone frostily above the hills and the moon seemed a small crescent in the vast heavens. But, as Miriam gazed upwards from the open door, one star more radiant than the rest lit up the sky over Bethlehem as though it were day. What was the meaning of it?

'Time for bed!' called her mother. 'Don't disturb Peter when you get in. I've just got him off to sleep.'

For they all slept in the one big bed which was a mattress covered with goatskin blankets on the raised part of the one-roomed house, out of the draughts. Baby Peter was wrapped in swaddling clothes so that he could not kick himself free from where he had been put or roll off. Father and James would be out all night on the hills in this wintry weather, watching that a pack of hungry wolves did not attack the flock lying secure in the little stone-walled sheep-fold they had built.

Mother came to bed but Miriam stayed awake, restless. At last she got up, slipped her mother's warm cloak over her woollen tunic and went outside. The strange star was still shining and it seemed to call to her, 'Come and see! Come and see!'

She had always been adventurous. And now, without fear, she untied the donkey, climbed onto his back from the low wall by the shed, and made for Bethlehem. As she approached the town she saw that the star was shining over a small stone out-house which housed the beasts of the local inn. She slid from the donkey and led him into the stable so strangely bathed in light.

There, in a manger on a bed of hay, lay a little baby, wrapped in swaddling clothes. His mother sat beside him humming an evening hymn. Her husband stood watching over them.

'Come in, little one,' he said. 'Behold the Saviour Jesus.'

The baby opened his eyes and as she gazed at him she knew that she would meet him again and one day he would give her her heart's desire.

A hand she recognized touched her shoulder. Her father was there with other shepherds, smiling happily. James shouted excitedly, 'We have seen wonders! Angels with bright wings singing glory to God and peace on earth!'

But I gave his mother a drink when she was thirsty, said Miriam to herself, and I'll bring her milk today.

© Sheila Forsdyke

The Christmas Good Samaritan

Take a parable told by Jesus, add a touch of seasonal flavour and dramatic flair, and you have a snappy sketch that an all-age group would relish presenting.

Narrator A little old lady was shuffling down the street with a plastic carrier bag of Christmas food.

Chorus (*Mime shuffling along.*)

Narrator When she was mugged by a gang.

Chorus   Gimme! (*Hold out hands.*)

Narrator   They pushed her over in the snow.

Chorus   (*Push*)

Narrator   And ran off with all her Christmas shopping.

Chorus   (*Sing, very badly and out of tune, just like hooligans*)

            'Jingle bells, jingle bells, jingle all the way . . .'

Narrator   Now, you'd have thought that at Christmas everyone would be rushing to help, wouldn't you?

Chorus   No! (*All shake heads.*)

Narrator   Well, there were plenty of people around who should have stopped to help.

Chorus   'Ello, 'ello, 'ello, what've we got 'ere?

            (*All bend knees like a policeman.*)

Narrator   But the policeman wanted to get back to the station for a . . .

Chorus   Mince pie. M-m-m-m!

            (*Rub tummy.*)

Narrator   Then there was Cinderella from the pantomime at the theatre. She didn't stop either.

Chorus   I'm late for rehearsals.

Narrator   There was the posh lady who did the flower arranging at church.

Chorus   (*Posh voice*) I can't be late for the carol service.

Narrator   There was Santa Claus from the grotto at the Co-op.

Chorus   I'm off for a nice cup of tea. Ho, ho, ho, ho, ho!

Narrator   There was the postman who'd been delivering cards since the crack of dawn.

Chorus   My feet are killing me.

Narrator   There was a busy mum, buying presents for her children.

Chorus   Can't stop. Too busy.

Narrator   Oh dear, isn't anyone going to stop and help the old lady?

            Then she heard someone singing.

Chorus   (*Sing, rather out of tune*)

            'I'm dreaming of a white Christmas . . .'

Narrator It was a drunk on his way home from the pub. But he stopped.

Chorus (*Everyone points unsteadily.*)

Narrator He helped the old lady up.

Chorus A-a-a-a-ah!

Narrator And gave her 20 pounds for her Christmas shopping. Then he took an enormous Christmas card out of his pocket and gave it to the old lady.

(*Two children hold up an enormous card.*)

Narrator Then he went off singing.

Chorus (*Sing*) 'We wish you a merry Christmas and a happy New Year!'

Narrator So, which one was the Christmas Good Samaritan?

© Jon Webster

13

The night before Christmas

This story captures all the magic of a special Christmas, seen through the eyes of a child. Definitely one that all the young at heart will treasure. It might also be read during a Christingle or crib service.

It was Christmas Eve, and outside the snow lay deep and still. Dan leant with his elbows on the window-sill at the far end of his room, looking at the big, pale moon climbing into the sky. Sometimes he thought it was like the single eye of a very old man, and at other times he thought that it resembled a polished white skull. The moon made everything clear and bright underneath, a strange colour that was eerie and unreal.

In the corner of Dan's room was a stack of presents as tall as himself, and there was even a little Christmas tree covered with brightly coloured lights and toys. There was money, too, from Grandpa and Grandma, and new games downstairs. But the strange thing was that now they had all come, he didn't really feel happy with them. He had all the toys he wanted and he couldn't think of anything he just had to buy. So he remained by the window, looking out at the hills rising up above the village and the great light that filled every hollow and valley.

All at once there came a knock at the front door downstairs. Dan held his breath and listened, as his mother's footsteps came out into the hall and she went to unlock the door.

'I've come to see Dan. I've got a surprise for him.' Dan recognized his Grandpa's voice and climbed from the window-ledge, drummed downstairs and ran into the hall.

'You're coming sledging with me, young man,' said Grandpa, and put into the boy's arms an old-fashioned wooden sledge that was all shiny and smooth, the colour of toffee. Dan was so surprised he didn't know what to say, but in a moment he found he had his coat and gloves on, and was out in the dead still December night.

'We're going right to the very top of the farm road,' Grandpa told him, and took hold of his hand. 'Come on, we'll get nice and warm if we walk quickly enough, I promise you.'

Dan was out of breath by the time they reached the end of the snowy track. But inside his gloves his fingers glowed red and warm just as his grandfather had promised. Now there was not a sound in all the world. The only signs of life were the sprinkling of gold and amber lights in among the hills. Dan wondered how far away they were. Maybe they were *hundreds* of miles away, as far as France or even America. Nobody could be *quite* sure.

'Now, we're ready. I'll get on first and you hold on as tight as you can.'

Dan did as his grandfather told him and sat at the back of the sledge. For a second nothing happened and the runners just made a deep grumbling sound and hardly moved. Then Grandpa pushed off again and very slowly the sledge started running down the track that shone with ice. Now they were going and the moon started darting in and out of the tops of the pine trees. Dan felt a strange lightness in his tummy and he clung on with all his strength. The sledge swung round the first bend and into a great dip. Dan opened his mouth to cry aloud but nothing happened; they just went on into a new corner and everything became fast and wonderful and strange. An owl floated over the track somewhere. Dan saw the flicker of a light in the trees, and the moon flashed past the pines faster and faster until Dan was out of breath and bits of snow were driving into his face so he could hardly see anything at all.

At the last minute, Grandpa did something wrong. The sledge went up in the air, and the two of them tumbled over onto the white verge as the sledge went running on into the moonlight. They both sat up, laughing, their cheeks red as holly berries.

'Look!' Grandpa said suddenly, 'and listen.'

Dan did. He saw the village down below in the valley, the glowing of the lights and fires from every house. Up above, the sky was filled as if with crystals, hundreds and hundreds of sharp stars flickering like sapphires and rubies.

'It could be Bethlehem,' Grandpa breathed gently. 'Can't you just imagine one of the stables on the edge of the village being where the baby Jesus was born?'

Dan nodded. He could, he could imagine it, and for a moment he really believed it was, and that he and Grandpa were on their way to find the strange new king that had come into the world. He thought again of all the presents he'd had and all the money and he felt sure that this was better than everything else put together. This was the real Christmas, the one you never got tired of or forgot.

Dan knew this was the Christmas he had been to Bethlehem, his very own Bethlehem, and he was so glad his Grandpa had taken him.

© Kenneth Steven

Crafts for Christmas

Christmas

To celebrate Christmas, why not have an activity session to make presents? The collection of the needed items will need to start well in advance. People of all ages could be encouraged to make the following:

A present to give someone else and/or a present for themselves

Simple presents to give and keep could include lavender bags or sachets of pot pourri, easy no-cook sweets in a decorated box, a calendar, Christmas-tree decorations, table decorations with a candle, packets of gift tags cut from old cards, decorated biscuits, bookmarks, decorated yoghurt pots as plant-pot holders, pencil holders, finger puppets and so on.

A present from a group of people to give to the church

A present from a group to the church could be a banner, a frieze of the Christmas story, home-made Christmas cards for those who can no longer come to church or who receive home communion, or a set of crib figures to set out in the church. The base for these last figures could be plastic bottles filled with water, with the lids glued on, or cardboard tubes stuffed with newspaper and stuck down. Use a newspaper ball as a head and cover with material and secure with an elastic band. Then dress the characters with suitably draped cloth.

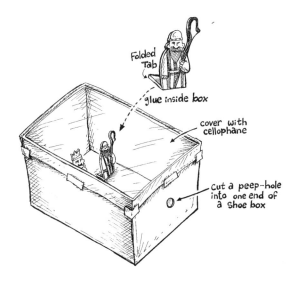

Folded Tab

glue inside box

cover with cellophane

Cut a peep-hole into one end of a shoe box

A home-made visual aid for exploring the greatest present the world has ever received

A visual aid for the Christmas story could be a crib scene in a shoe box. For this, cut out pictures of all the characters from old Christmas cards. Leave a tab to fold under to stick the character to the box. Cut a peep-hole into one end of the box, arrange and stick down the characters, and put straw on the floor. Then cover the box with Cellophane and look through the peep-hole.

© Betty Pedley and Joan Chapman

Are you ready for Christmas?

Cast

Mum, Dad, Two children, Voice

A family is preparing for Christmas. Dad is reading his paper. Mum is checking through her list. Children are decorating the tree. There is also a voice off-stage, which, one by one, the characters hear.

Mum   (*Reading list*) Right now, let's check we have everything. Turkey, cranberry sauce, stuffing, potatoes, sprouts, carrots. . . . (*To Dad*) Will you prepare the veg for me, love?

Dad   Uh. (*Non-committal grunt.*)

Mum   Well, will you?

Dad   Yeah – when I've finished reading my paper.

Mum   Christmas pudding . . . cream . . .

Child 1   (*Interrupting*) Oh no, Mum – can't we have custard? I don't like cream.

Mum	We'll see. Now, where was I?
Voice	You've forgotten something.
Mum	Who said that?
Child 1	What Mum?
Mum	Oh nothing. Cream, After Eights, chocolates, crackers . . .
Child 2	Can we have those with the special magic tricks in them?
Mum	Not this time.
Voice	You've still forgotten something.
Mum & Dad	Who said that? (*Slight pause, then shrug and continue.*)
Dad	Did you get my beer? And the nuts and my cigarettes? I can't last the Christmas season without them.
Mum	Yes.
Child 1	What about mince pies, popcorn and crisps?
Child 2	And pop – cherryade's my favourite. You did get the TV guide, didn't you, Mum? I don't want to miss Back to the Future.
Voice	You've forgotten something.
Mum	Oh yes, wrapping paper, cards, party poppers and . . .
Voice	Hey, wait a minute!
All	Who said that?
Voice	I did. I'm the still small voice.
All	Well, what have we forgotten?
Voice	Jesus. He's the most important part of Christmas.
Dad	Well, yes – I know he was born in Bethlehem and all that story that goes along with it – but, well, it's not relevant today, is it?
Voice	That's just where you're wrong. Jesus is still looking for a place to stay today. A heart where he will be welcome to come and live as your Saviour and Lord.
	(*Pause. Then the voice addresses the audience*)
Voice	Are you ready for Christmas?
	(*All freeze.*)

The little glass horse

The true value of giving presents at Christmas can often be lost. This story for younger children shows how important it is to give, whatever the present might be.

It was small. It had thin spindly legs and a head that was a little too large. It was made of clear glass but inside the glass was a centre of brightly coloured material, like the marbles that her brother played with. It was a little glass horse. Gemma thought it was the most beautiful thing that she had ever seen.

Gemma's mum liked watching horses on television. Gemma knew that she would like the little glass horse.

'How much is it?' she asked the lady at the stall.

'What, dear?' asked the lady.

'The little glass horse.'

'25p,' said the lady.

'Oh,' said Gemma. She only had 20p. 'I want to buy it for my mum, for Christmas', she went on, 'but I have only got 20p left.'

The lady did not seem to be listening. Gemma tried again.

'My mum likes horses,' she said.

'Yes, dear,' said the lady.

'I want to buy that horse as a present for her.'

'How much money have you got?'

'20p.'

'Oh, very well, you can have it for 20p. Shall I put it in a bag for you?'

'Thank you. Yes please,' said Gemma as she handed over her last coin. Carefully she took the bag. She knew that glass could break easily. She knew that she must be careful to keep the present a secret.

Somehow the horse survived the journey home in the car, then being hidden in a drawer in Gemma's room and finally being wrapped up. It is difficult to wrap up a horse, even a glass one.

In Gemma's family Christmas presents were put round the tree during Christmas Eve and were not opened until after lunch on Christmas Day.

On Christmas Eve Gemma placed her mum's present, the little glass horse, carefully in a safe place by the tree. She was very excited. She knew that her mum would love the little glass horse. Gemma knew it was the best present that she could ever give her mum. It was perfect. She wanted to see her mum's face when she opened the present.

After lunch on Christmas Day everyone sat down in a circle. The youngest child in the family had a special job to do. It was their task to take the presents from under the tree and give them to the person to whom they were addressed. This was now the job for Gemma's little brother. Gemma had done it for two Christmases, but now she was too old and it was her brother's turn. Actually the youngest person was Aunt Clare's new baby, but you could not ask a new baby to carry presents round the room; that would be silly.

Gemma's brother took the job very seriously and carefully. Everyone watched each present being opened and said nice things about it when they saw what the present was.

Gemma felt bubbly with excitement. She knew that her present for her mum was perfect. She could almost hear everyone saying how nice it was.

It was no one's fault really. Gemma's brother was being very careful. It was just that Aunt Clare's new baby suddenly yelled just as he was stepping over Uncle John's new golf bag. Gemma's brother tripped. The horse, in its wrapping paper, fell on the floor and Gemma's brother fell on top of it. There was a scrunch, followed by a silence. Gemma's brother yelled and was picked up and comforted. Gemma looked at the sad squashed shape that had been the perfect present for her mum. Big tears started to form in her eyes. It had been perfect and now it was smashed. She cried.

Later, when she had been comforted, she tried to tell her mum what the little glass horse had been like, but she could not describe it properly. At last her mum said, 'When the shops are open again after Christmas we will go to look for another little glass horse, so you can give that to me instead.'

'But it did not come from a shop.'

'I know, dear, but there is a place in town which sells lots of glass animals. We can find one there.'

Gemma and her mum did go to the special shop and they did find a little glass horse that was very like the one that Gemma had found on the stall. They took it home and mum put it in a very special place on the mantel piece. Mum said that she was very pleased with it and so everything was all right. Gemma knew that it was not quite perfect because it was not the one that she had found.

Years later, when Gemma was quite grown up and had her own home, she was visiting her mum one day. She noticed the little glass horse still in its special place on the mantelpiece.

'Why do you still keep this old thing here?' she asked her mum.

'Because you gave it to me. It was so special for you that it made it special for me.'

A thought struck Gemma. 'Mum do you like horses?'

'Not much. I prefer cats. You can cuddle a cat. But that little glass horse is very special. You gave it to me.'

© David W. Lankshear

Jesus' birthday party

An all-age service

This action-packed service requires a certain amount of preparation beforehand, but it is well worth the effort. The aim of this material is to incorporate elements of a traditional party-style celebration, which would be recognized and identified as such by an all-age congregation, into an act of Christian worship.

In preparation

There are a number of things that will need to be prepared in advance.

Food   Star-shaped biscuits, baby-in-the-manger sandwiches (a slice of French bread with two cheese circles to make a 'baby'), crisps, mince pies, drinks and so on.

Crackers   Make crackers using cardboard tubes, tissue or crêpe paper. Put inside snaps bought from a party shop, a sweet or tiny toy and a Christmas message instead of a joke.

A card   Make a large birthday card for Jesus ready for everyone to sign.

A cake   This should preferably be a real cake which can be cut and distributed at the end, but an artificial one is fine. The main requirement is that it should have candles which can be lit.

A present   Wrap up a large box, big enough for a child to get inside. Make sure you leave one end open. Arrange with a suitable child that they will get in the box secretly at the right moment during the service.

Songs   The service includes some simple songs to nursery tunes. It would help to have the words on an OHP or flip-chart.

A game   You will need a large jigsaw type game. See in the service for details of just what is needed.

A stable   Make an area of the church into a stable scene large enough to accommodate the number of children you expect to come.

Welcome

Song   'While shepherds watched' (SF 602).

Leader   We begin our story on a hilltop. We've sung about the shepherds, now I need your help in telling their story.

(Ask some children to come to the front and put them in very simple costumes to help you tell the story of the shepherds and their visit to the stable.)

What a wonderful story the shepherds had to tell! The same message is for us today. We too can meet Jesus. That is the reason why we have met here today.

The shepherds visited Jesus on his birthday, or possibly the day after, and we have gathered to hold a celebration and party for Jesus.

When we are going to have a party, what do we need?

(You need to make sure you get all the following items on a list, from the answers given.)
- food
- crackers
- a card
- a cake
- a present
- songs to sing
- people to come

So, which of these things have we got? *(Hold up each type of thing as you ask about it.)*

Leader   Is there any food?

Answer   Yes!

Leader   Are there any crackers?

Answer   Yes!

Leader   Is there a card?

Answer   Yes!

(*Send a child round the congregation, passing the card round for everyone to sign.*)

Leader   Is there any food?

Answer   Yes!

Leader   Is there a present?

Answer   Yes!

Leader   We do need songs to sing. Here are some you might know the tunes of very well. (*Display the words*) We'll learn these to use later.

1.   Hear the news the angels bring, (x3)
    God sent his son Jesus.
    (*Tune: 'Skip to my Lou'.*)

2.   O joyful Christmastime,
    O joyful Christmastime,
    We're so glad baby Jesus came,
    At joyful Christmastime.
    The donkey and the sheep were there . . .
    The shepherds heard the news . . .
    (*Tune: 'Ring o' roses'.*)

3.   A Saviour's been born,
    Hurry up, we can go
    To see baby Jesus.
    God sent us his son.
    (*Tune: 'Happy birthday'.*)

Leader   Are there people to come to this party?

Answer   Yes!

Carol   'Once in royal David's city' (SF 438).

(*Send two adults to the stable as Mary and Joseph with simple cloth draped around their heads and shoulders. Tell the congregation you are now going to journey to Bethlehem. Have some appropriate music playing as the congregation walks around the church following a leader. While this is happening, secretly send the child to climb into the present box.*

The congregation come to the stable and the children go and sit in the straw while the adults gather round.)

Song   'Hear the news the angels sing' ('*Skip to my Lou*')

Carol   'Away in a manger' (SF 36).

Leader   Now we're going to play a game.

(Bring out a board with five large jigsaw pieces to stick on. Each piece has a message on it about the Christ child from the prophecy of Isaiah and the message of the angels. Get some older children to put it together on the board. It will end up with a round gap in the middle.)

Let's read what the messages say. They are all things that the Bible says about Jesus:

'unto us a child is born';
'he will be called wonderful, counsellor';
'you will find a baby . . . lying in a manger';
'good news of great joy';
'a saviour has been born to you'.

But whatever we say, however many words we use, there is something missing if we don't have the piece in the middle.

(Get one of the older members of the congregation to come and put on the missing jigsaw circle, a picture of baby Jesus.)

Prayer   *(Pray simply, asking Jesus to be the centre of our lives. Or have prayers prepared by teenagers and older children on the same theme.)*

Song   'O joyful Christmastime' ('*Ring o' roses*')

Card and cake   *(Offer the card containing all the signatures by laying it in the straw. Then light the candles on the cake.)*

Song   'A Saviour's been born' ('*Happy birthday*')

Present *(Lift the present and put it into the stable. The child bursts out. Explain that we are here to celebrate, but also to bring ourselves, the gift of our lives, to Jesus.)*

Carol   'In the bleak mid-winter' (SF 243).

Final prayers and blessing

Carol   'Hark the herald angels sing' (SF 155).

(During the last verse, move to an area of the church where crackers, mince pies, star biscuits and other food is set out for everyone to enjoy.)

© Betty Pedley

Epiphany

Gifts for the giver

This sketch is ideal for first-time performers as well as experienced dramatists. It requires a minimum number of props and can be performed equally well on either a large stage, or a small space at the front of the church.

Cast

Narrator and three 'wise' men: Nigel, Dave and Jeremy

Set

Three chairs facing sideways towards stage right.

Presents, Bible and three pairs of sunglasses in a pile at front stage centre.

Narrator This is the story of the three kings . . .

All three (*Off-stage singing*) Well it's one for the money, two for the show, three to get ready now go let's go . . . (*a la Elvis!*)

Narrator Not those sort of kings. Let's start again. This is the story of the three wise men. After Jesus was born in Bethlehem in Judea, wise men from the East came to Jerusalem to worship the one who had been born King of the Jews.

All three (*All three enter stage right suitably dressed as kings, Dave carrying clipboard and large feather 'quill'.*)

Nigel Ready for the off?

Dave (*Consults list*) Presents?

Jeremy (*Counts presents*) All present and correct!

Dave (*Groans and ticks list*) Prophecies?

Jeremy (*Holds up Bible*) Prophecies.

Dave (*Ticks list.*)

Nigel Sunglasses?

Dave Sunglasses?!

Nigel This is one seriously bright star we're talking about!

Jeremy (*Locates sunglasses and hands them out*) Sunglasses.

Dave (*Ticks list*) Right, off we go.

All three (*All three pick up their presents and immediately do the following*)

Nigel (*Wanders round as if looking for something and then exits stage right.*)

Dave (*Disposes of clipboard stage right, sits on chair facing stage left and watches the following action bemused.*)

Jeremy (*Grabs Bible, looks up a 'prophecy' and puts it back. Then, to the tune of 'Yankey Doodle Dandy'*)

La La La La La La . . .

Narrator	What are you doing?
Jeremy	Riding to Jerusalem on a donkey.
Narrator	No, no, no, the baby does that later – 30 years later! You ride that camel.
Jeremy	(*Making way to centre chair and sitting on it facing stage left*)
	Oops sorry, wrong prophecy.
Nigel	(*Enters stage right*) Has anyone seen my camel?
	(*Other two point to remaining chair which he sits on facing stage left.*)
All three	(*Over-acting by all three during following narration. All three put on sunglasses. Dave and Jeremy point stage left while Nigel points stage right, realizes his mistake and points 'east' looking embarrassed.*)
Narrator	The wise men had seen Jesus' star in the east and had brought gifts to give to the baby king.
All three	(*Then turn heads to stage front with wide grins, holding presents out for everyone to see and freeze in that position for a couple of seconds.*)
All three	(*All three mime stopping camels and dismounting, then take off sunglasses and put presents on 'camels'.*)
Dave	What are you going to give him then?
Nigel	Well, I thought I'd get in early and avoid the Christmas rush.
Dave	Well – what did you buy?
Nigel	Frankincense.
Jeremy	(*Sarcastically*) Oh, I could see there would be a big demand for frankincense this time of the year!
Nigel	OK then, what did you get?
Jeremy	(*Defensively*) Myrrh.
Dave	Perfume? (*with a French accent*) Myrrh – not very macho is it?
Jeremy	All right clever cloggs, what did you buy?
Dave	Er – gold actually.
Nigel	Don't you think a rubber duck or a cuddly toy might have been more appropriate?
Dave	(*Aside to congregation*) It would definitely have been cheaper!
Nigel	(*To narrator*) Exactly where are we going with these presents anyway?
Narrator	Look at the prophecy.

All three   (*All study a Bible passage closely.*)

Narrator   But you Bethlehem, in the land of Judah, are by no means least among the rulers of Judah; for out of you will come a ruler . . .

Nigel   (*Interrupting*) Wait, wait, I've got one! (*Rummages for ruler.*)

Narrator   Got one what?

Nigel   (*Produces twelve-inch ruler*) A ruler!

Narrator   Not that sort of ruler.

Nigel   Oh . . . sorry. (*Puts ruler away.*)

Narrator   May I continue?

Nigel   Yes, sorry.

Narrator   For out of you will come a ruler who will be the shepherd of my people Israel.

Dave   Shepherd (*Thinks*). I got one, I got one. What do you call a sheep with no legs? (*Reply of 'a cloud' from the congregation*) Oh, you've heard it before.

All three   (*All three put on sunglasses and stand and stare to the 'east' – stage left – until the following narration is finished*)

Narrator   The star they had seen in the east went ahead of them until it stopped over the place where the child was.

(*All three suddenly realize they are going to be left behind.*)

Jeremy   Hey wait for us!

(*All three pick up presents and gallop off stage left on 'camels'. All three disrobe from their kings' gear, revealing matching clothing underneath.*)

Narrator   On coming to the house, they saw the child with his mother Mary, and they bowed down and worshipped him. Then they opened their treasures and presented him with their gifts.

(*During following narrations each enters stage left with imaginary gift which is placed on stage centre. They turn to face congregation and do appropriate mime.*)

Dave   (*Mime ending on one knee upstage right. Freeze.*)

Narrator   Gold for the king of kings, who left his place of glory to be born in a stable, and gave of himself to teach, heal and serve. Jesus the servant king.

Jeremy   (*Mime ending in crucified position, upstage centre. Freeze.*)

Narrator   Myrrh for the baby, born to die, despised, rejected, mocked and beaten, who willingly gave his life to the cruel death of crucifixion.

Nigel   (*Mime ending in offering of imaginary gift to congregation, upstage left. Freeze.*)

Narrator   Frankincense to worship the Lord who rose from death to conquer sin, bringing forgiveness to all who will ask and receive his gift of salvation.

© Sue Hardgrave

The star

An Epiphany all-age service

As everyone arrives in church, give them a white cardboard star about six inches in diameter and a pencil.

Welcome
Opening prayer

All	O God, we have come to your house today to worship you.
	We remember that you are here with us now,
	Help us to pray to you,
	Help us to praise you,
	Help us to learn about you,

Bless us and our service today,

And when we leave your house

We pray that you will not leave us,

For Jesus Christ's sake. Amen.

Offertory hymn   'As with gladness men of old' (HAMR 79).

Offertory prayer

All   O God, we know that you are the giver of all good things,

We offer this money back to you,

To be used by your Church.

May it help to build your kingdom,

Both in this parish and beyond,

For the sake of Jesus Christ,

Who told us to preach the gospel everywhere. Amen.

Confession and absolution

Leader   All of us sometimes fail to do the things we should do,

All of us say and do things we know to be wrong,

Let us tell God how sorry we are,

And ask him to forgive us.

All   O God, our loving Father

We know that you forgive those who honestly confess their sins.

We ask you to forgive us

For the good things we have failed to do,

And for the wrong things we have done.

We have often broken your rules,

We have often hurt other people,

We have forgotten the teachings of your Son Jesus Christ.

All these things we now confess to you,

We ask your forgiveness,

And we ask you to help us live better lives day by day.

For Jesus Christ's sake. Amen.

Leader   May almighty God have mercy on us,
forgive us all our sins,
through our Lord Jesus Christ,
strengthen us in all goodness,
and by the power of the Holy Spirit
bring us to eternal life. Amen.

Readings   Micah 5.2

Matthew 2.1-12

Creed   (*Sung to the tune of 'Onward Christian soldiers'*)

1.   I believe in God most high,
He made heaven and earth,
Father-like he's loved me
Ever since my birth.

2.   I believe in Jesus Christ,
Son of God from heaven,
He who died upon the cross
And rose to life again.

3.   I believe the Holy Spirit
Comes to us today,
Helps us live like Jesus,
Helps us work and pray.

The peace

Hymn 'In the stars his handiwork I see' (JP 112).

Presentation: the star

Leader We are going to explore now one possible explanation about the star that appeared over Bethlehem. We don't know for sure what happened, but this is one idea.

Narrator 1 In the Land of Two Rivers, about 45 miles north of Babylon, at the point where the Euphrates and Tigris come closest together in what is now Iraq, there was an ancient university town called Sippar. For at least 1,200–1,500 years before Jesus was born, there had been an astronomical observatory there.

(Leader then asks the congregation what astronomers do. Give out a sign saying SIPPAR for someone to hold and ask for volunteer astronomers. Give them binoculars, cardboard-roll telescopes and tea-towel and hairband head-dresses.)

Narrator 2 In 600 BC Nebuchadnezzar conquered Jerusalem and transplanted many of the Jews to Babylon, where they continued to live even up to the time of Jesus' birth. As many Jews excelled in maths, it seems reasonable to assume that some of them studied in the astronomy schools. For all that time – 1,500 years – a daily record had been kept of the movements of the sun and moon, and particularly of the Wanderers, the planets that can be seen to move, against the background of the fixed stars.

(Give out clipboards to the astronomers to record movements, and ask everyone to hold up their stars.)

Narrator 1 Now, we are particularly interested in the Wanderers, because one of these is Jupiter, indicating a king, a very great king.

(Give out a huge cardboard circle Jupiter, with its name and 'The King' written on it. It is worth giving this planet, and the next one, to people who have rehearsed beforehand.)

Narrator 2   Another Wanderer is Saturn, the protecting star of Israel.

(Give out Saturn, with its name and 'Israel' written on it. Ask Jupiter and Saturn to wander around the church, with everyone holding up their stars and the astronomers watching and recording movements.)

Narrator 1   Now in order to find something in the stars you have to know what you are looking for, and when and where to watch. Eight hundred and five years previously, a triple meeting of planets in the sky had been recorded, but this time the astronomers, probably Jews who had read the Scriptures, knew how to interpret what was happening in the sky. It is still the custom today, when an unusual thing is to be seen in the sky, for astronomers to arrange an expedition to watch it.

According to our calendar, it was in May, 7 BC, that Jupiter and Saturn, the two largest planets, called the Wanderers, had come within one degree of each other in the part of the sky representing the zodiacal sign of Pisces which indicated Mediterranean lands such as Judaea. It was in the eastern sky just before daybreak.

(Hold a large star behind the two planets now next to each other in the chancel – the east.)

Narrator 1   On 5 October that same year, the two planets came together again, this time at midnight, directly overhead.

(Hold large star with planets in the centre of the church.)

Narrator 2   Now, soon after this, the Babylonian astronomers set off from the East to follow the star, because they knew it would appear again.

(Give some astronomers crowns, the planets wander again.)

Narrator 1   Nowhere in the Bible does it say there were three wise men who came from the East, it could have been a dozen. It is highly unlikely that only three men would make such a trip, and even if there were only three astronomers, they would have had many servants. They were not actually kings, but were men of great importance, so we will let them keep their crowns. Moreover, they were transporting a very valuable cargo, so may well have had armed guards as well as servants.

(Ask for some volunteer servants and guards. Ask what the gifts were, and give out three for the guards to carry.)

Narrator 2   So there must have been quite a caravan that headed off on the 1,000-mile journey. The Bible mentions no camels, by the way, but it is a reasonable guess that camels were used, although horses and wagons were often used for such long trips. They would have travelled about 20 miles per day.

Narrator 1 And now, for the third time, 56 days later, on 1 December, the planets were once more in conjunction in the south-west, in the sunset sky.

(The planets and large star move to the south-west corner of the church, Jupiter one way and Saturn the other, with the star hidden until the two planets come together. Send the astronomers with their helpers on the journey from the front of the church to the south-west corner.)

Narrator 2 As soon as the travelling caravan was settled in Jerusalem, they began to ask among the local people about the great king – indicated by Jupiter, born to the Jews – indicated by Saturn, in the land of Judea – indicated by the part of the sky in which the coming together of the Wanderers was happening.

Narrator 1 Please note that there was no star like a searchlight standing over Bethlehem. Herod had seen nothing, nor had anyone else in Palestine. Only the astronomers, who knew what, when and where to watch, realized something special had happened in the sky.

Narrator 2 We know the story. Herod asked his scribes what the Scriptures said. That was an easy one to answer, and we have had the reading this morning. For 500 years it had plainly said in Micah: 'But you, Bethlehem . . . out of you will come for me, one who will be ruler over Israel.'

Narrator 1 So that was where, Bethlehem. After coming so far, the wise men decided that there was still time before dark to go such a little way. Finally, after all those months of uncertain anticipation, they would actually see the child. As they went out of the south gate of Jerusalem, like all good astronomers they were watching the sunset sky. Suddenly, in the glow, and apparently right over Bethlehem, the town they were heading for, there was the evening star.

Narrator 2 For Saturn and Jupiter had been joined by Mars.

(Give out Mars, and a sign 'Bethlehem', and send them to join the other planets.)

Narrator 1 The three planets together made a great blazing light, the star. It was now February in 6 BC

(Hold star in front of the three planets.)

Narrator 2   And from Matthew, our other reading this morning, we hear: 'On coming to the house, they saw the child' – note that it wasn't a baby – 'with his mother Mary, and they bowed down and worshipped him.'

Narrator 1   So the star-gazers may well have been from Sippar in Babylon, Jews who had read the Scriptures and could understand what they saw, when they saw it, and who knew where to go to see the fulfilment of the Scriptures.

Song   A choir of children might perform a modern carol here, such as The 'Calypso carol' or 'If I'd been there'.

Hymn   'O Worship the Lord' (HAMR 77).

Prayers   (*Ask the congregation to spend a few minutes writing on their small stars anything they wished to pray for. The stars are then collected by a few children and pinned on boards covered in black crêpe paper, as the night sky. Some, or all of the prayers can then be read aloud. Finish with the Lord's Prayer.*)

Final hymn   'The first nowell'. (SF 529, HON 477). (*During this hymn, the boards, planets, star and signs for Sippar and Bethlehem are put in front of the altar.*)

The blessing

Note

The background information for the presentation in this service comes from E.L.C. Austin, *The Gift of Christmas – A Closer Look*, Baker Book House.

© Jenny Loxston

The story of the fourth wise man

This sketch was adapted from the version of the legend in A Third Book of 101 School Assembly Stories, *Foulsham, 1987. It is an intriguing story about an imaginary wise man, who missed travelling with the traditional three. There are a number of non-speaking parts in this sketch, making it ideal for performance by groups of children.*

Cast

Narrator	Crowd 1
Artaban	Crowd 2
Jew	Girl
Woman	Voice
Captain	Choir
Characters for nativity scene	

Narrator	In the days when Jesus was born, there were wise men who studied the stars. One of these men was known as Artaban. One night, he saw to his excitement that the planets and stars had come together in such a way that it meant a great king was to be born among the Jews. At once, he contacted his fellow astrologers, Caspar, Melchior and Balthazar, and agreed to join them in a journey to find this new king.
	First, he sold everything he had, and bought three jewels, a ruby, a sapphire and a pearl, as gifts for the king.
	Then, every night, he studied the sky, waiting for the sign to appear.
Artaban	At last! I can see the star. How I have longed for this moment! I am ready to go to the meeting place to find the others. Together we shall find the promised king.
Narrator	So Artaban set off past the ruins of Babylon and through forests of palm trees towards the desert.
	(*A man is lying across the path. He is moaning and crying for help.*)
Artaban	What is that sound?
	(*He goes over and kneels by the man.*)
	Marsh fever! A serious complaint, and this man is a Jew. What shall I do? I have the skills to save his life, but it will take time and the others will go on without me.
	(*He stands up and turns away. Then he turns back again.*)
	Yes, to save him would be an act of love and love is of God.
	(*He kneels down and gives him medicine, and comforts him.*)
Jew	(*Weakly*) How is it that you, an Arab, are caring for me, a Jew?
Artaban	(*Sighing*) To use my skills as an act of love.
Jew	But what are you doing here in the desert?
Artaban	I am following the star which will lead me to the King of the Jews.
Jew	I can give you nothing for all you have done for me, but I think I can help you in your quest. According to our Scriptures, the Jewish Messiah will be born in Bethlehem. You must seek him there.
Narrator	It was after midnight when Artaban reached the meeting place. There was no sign of his friends. Only a note remained, scrawled on a piece of parchment. They had gone on without him. Sadly, Artaban returned to Babylon to sell his ruby and buy the provisions he needed for his lonely trip.

(*While the narrator speaks, the three wise men approach the stable, offer their gifts and depart. The choir sing 'The Coventry Carol'. During this carol, Mary, Joseph and the baby Jesus come forward and go to the side.*)

Narrator   At last he reached Bethlehem. The place was strangely quiet.

(*Enter woman with a baby. She sits down and starts singing a lullaby. Artaban approaches softly. He knocks on the door.*)

Woman   Come in.

Artaban   I wonder if you can help me. Has there been an unusual birth in this town recently?

Woman   Well, yes. A few days ago, three richly dressed strangers suddenly appeared from nowhere. They were asking to see the King of the Jews.

Artaban   Where did all this take place? Are they there still?

Woman   No, they went as suddenly as they had come.

Artaban   And the baby?

Woman   He and his parents disappeared too. They must have left in the middle of the night, for no one saw them go.

(*Sounds of clashing swords, screams, and cries of: 'Not my baby! No! No!' The woman stands up and holds her baby tightly to her. Artaban stands in front of her. There is a loud hammering at the door.*)

Captain	Open up, in the name of Herod the King! Bring out your babies to be slaughtered. The king's command must be obeyed.

(Artaban reaches in his pocket for his sapphire and holds it out to the captain of the guard. He slowly reaches forward and snatches it. Then he turns to go.)

Captain March on, soldiers! There is no baby in this house.

(The sound of marching, loud at first and then dying away.)

Artaban My second gift is gone.

Woman God will bless you for saving the life of my little one. May he be with you in your travels.

(Artaban touches her arm, and then turns and walks slowly away. The woman goes to the side, humming to her baby as she goes.)

Narrator For nearly 30 years, Artaban wandered from country to country, always searching for the king, until at last, as an old man, he journeyed to Jerusalem. It was Passover time and the streets were crowded with people.

(Enter people talking excitedly to each other, and all surging in the same direction.)

Artaban Where are you all going?

Crowd 1 We are off to Golgotha to the crucifixion.

Crowd 2 Yes, they are putting a man called Jesus of Nazareth to death because he claimed to be the King of the Jews.

Artaban *(Excitedly)* Why do I suddenly feel strange? Could this be the king I have spent my life searching for? Will I be in time to offer him comfort, or even to save his life?

(Enter soldiers holding a girl. She pulls herself free and throws herself down at Artaban's feet.)

Girl *(Desperately)* Please, please save me, sir. I am from your country. My father was a businessman, but he is in debt, and so I must be sold as a slave.

Artaban *(Sadly to himself)* I have only one jewel left. Should I pay the girl's ransom with this pearl or keep it for the king? To save this girl would be an act of love and love is of God, so this is what I must do.

(Artaban takes the pearl from his pocket and slowly places it in her outstretched hands.)

Artaban   Here is your ransom, my child. It is the last of the treasures that I was saving for the king.

(The lights dim, and there is the sound of thunder. The crowd sway and then kneel to one side. Artaban stands in the centre, as if gazing up at the cross.)

Voice   Truly I say to you. In as much as you did this for one of the least of these my brothers, you have done it for me.

(Artaban slowly kneels.)

Artaban   My search is over. My treasures have been accepted. I have found the king.

(Choir sing softly the first two verses of 'When I survey the wondrous cross' When I survey the wondrous cross, while the crowd slowly go back to their places, leaving Artaban still kneeling before the cross. Towards the end of the second verse, he too gets up and walks slowly away, still looking back as he does so.)

The adventure of three mice

This read-aloud Epiphany tale, inspired by verses from Isaiah, sees the story of the kings from a new angle.

This is a tale about some of the adventures of three mice who lived in different countries beyond the sea, where days are hot and long.

One of the mice lived in the palace of a king, and his furry coat had a pinkish colour. It suited him with his brown eyes. Now there was a large cat in the palace who used to try and catch him. This made him very frightened, so the little mouse used to play in the stable where the camels lived. He was happy there, and the camels never harmed him. At night, he would curl up in the bottom of a saddle-bag and sleep there.

One evening there was a great commotion and excited voices calling out, 'The star, the star – it's time to go, we must follow the star!' And before the Little Pink

Mouse could utter a squeak, the tall king had picked up the very saddle-bag where he was sleeping, climbed onto a camel and was off.

The little mouse didn't know what to do, so he went fast asleep until he could think. It was warm in the saddle-bag and there was straw to eat. They had only travelled a little way, when the king and his servants stopped. The mouse peeped out and saw the camels drinking from a nearby pool. Then there were voices and Little Pink Mouse thought he recognized a new one. Yes! It was his master's royal friend, who often used

to visit. The two kings were going to travel together. He heard them say, 'The star, the star, we must follow the star!'

They rode on quickly now, and seemed to be in a great hurry. They talked about meeting a third king. The mouse began to wonder how many kings were going to follow the star – and when he would get out of the saddle-bag for a proper breath of fresh air.

At last it was daylight and as there were no stars to be seen, they all stopped on the edge of a wood and rested. They opened their bags to get something to eat, and Little Pink Mouse smelt crumbs. He ventured out to have a meal too.

As he was happily nibbling he heard a tiny squeak, and a little yellow head appeared from a hole in the other king's saddle-bag. A mouse. He was very surprised indeed, but there were plenty of crumbs to share, and they were tastier ones than they usually had – even in royal palaces. Little Pink Mouse and Little Yellow Mouse ate and chatted, but they did not want to get left behind. After all, they couldn't be sure where they would get their next meal. And, with all this excitement about a star, they really wanted to see where it led. So they scuttled back into their saddle-bags.

This time, the kings rode faster than ever. It was dark now and they could see the star. Little Pink Mouse and Little Yellow Mouse were just settling down to sleep, when the camels suddenly stopped again. The mice looked out and saw a large building, which in the starlight looked like yet another palace. There, waiting by an arched gate, was another camel with another king just climbing onto his seat. Little Pink Mouse knew it must be a king because of the special kind of seat.

He did not get much sleep that night because the kings made their camels ride so quickly over a sandy desert. The star was brighter than ever and seemed to be always beckoning them on further. After a long time, the kings slowed down and stopped to rest and talk. Little Pink Mouse and Little Yellow Mouse heard them saying they were going to see a new king. He was still only a baby, but would rule the whole world one day and bring peace to everyone. The mice did not know what that meant, but hoped it might be something to do with cats not catching mice and hurting them any more.

Each of the kings brought out beautiful, expensive presents to give to the new baby king. The two mice were very curious, so they got as near as they could to have a good look. Little Pink Mouse's eyes nearly popped out of his head when he saw his own king's present of glittering gold. It was even more beautiful than the things he had seen in the palace.

The second king said he had brought the best he could, and even before he unwrapped it the mice could smell that it was frankincense. At that moment, it had a faint perfume, but they knew that once it was burning it would have a strong sweet smell.

By this time, the two little mice felt they wanted to give something to the new king, especially if he was going to make sure that one day mice would be safe from cats. They quickly got to work. Little Yellow Mouse said he would nibble through the string on the parcel of frankincense, to make it easier for the baby hands to untie.

Little Pink Mouse said, 'Well, if it is for a king, I shall make a crown.' And with a bit of help from Little Yellow Mouse, he made one from straw in the saddle-bag.

They were feeling quite pleased with themselves, and had got to know each other well, when the third king spoke about the present he had brought. He said quietly: 'I have here a jar of very precious ointment called myrrh, which has a sweet scent. I brought it because I know that the new king will have to suffer and die to bring us peace. It is rather a sad gift.' The three kings looked at it, but they did not fully understand.

While they were wondering about this special gift, a squeaky sob was heard, and the two mice saw, to their surprise, a very small orange mouse hiding near the third king. They heard him say: 'I have nothing to give the new king – only a tear' and they saw it drop right onto the myrrh. Little Pink Mouse and Little Yellow Mouse tried to comfort him, and they all decided to slip down together into the third king's saddle-bag. There they slept until morning.

When they woke, it was not quite light. The kings and the mice tidied themselves and rode off with their presents. Now they could all see the bright star shining, and at last it had stopped moving. They were in a little village with white stone houses everywhere. It was called Bethlehem.

The star shone over one house, so the kings got down from their camels and went towards the open door. They left their saddle-bags just inside, and took out their gifts to offer the baby king. He was playing on a rug with a beautiful, big cat. Every time he stroked the cat, it made a gentle, soothing sound, and seemed to say, 'Sleep, little king of all the beasts, sleep.'

The mice looked round, and were surprised to see a king in such a small place. His mother had a wonderful face. She looked lovingly at her son and said, 'His name is Jesus.' There was a tall, smiling man standing by them.

The three kings each took out the presents they had brought, and gave them to the baby king. Then the cat opened one eye and caught sight of Little Pink Mouse, Little Yellow Mouse and Little Orange Mouse. They were terrified and thought he might spring at them. But he grinned peacefully and looked so pleased to see them that they were not afraid any more. So they quickly got out of their hiding place, and Little Pink Mouse left his straw crown beside the present of gold. By now, Little Orange Mouse's tear had dried on the gift of myrrh, and the string that the Little Yellow Mouse had nibbled through was crumpled on the floor. It really had helped the baby to unwrap the present.

They were all happy together. They were sure that one day cats and mice would always live in peace with each other like this because of this wonderful new king. They let out high squeaks of pleasure, and clapped their paws. The cat just yawned.

How sad the three mice were when they had to set off home. The journey back was not nearly so exciting without the star to follow. But Little Pink Mouse, Little Yellow Mouse and Little Orange Mouse were very tired, and curled up and dreamt of their adventures.

© Phyllis A. Jackson

Three kings

*This poem would be particularly suitable for use with older children
and in all-age groups.*

Out of wintry shadows
wind sped like an arrow,
earth and water froze.

Albert wheeled his barrow,
leaning on his load.
'Christmas Day tomorrow.'

'On the downs it snowed,'
cried George, 'it's coming soon.'
Frank looked up the road.

That dark afternoon
a stranger walked ahead
haloed by the moon.

He half turned: 'Peace', he said.
Wind dropped. Like a sign
a star rose up and led

that moment out of time,
as if his gentle call
made earth and heaven rhyme.

Like a miracle
George, Frank and Albert felt
drawn into his will.

Lamplight seemed to melt,
with a wild grace stars
circled down to pelt

wheelbarrow and cars.
The three men hid their eyes
as love shook off its bars

and earth met paradise.
He left them in the falling
snow, with memories

too strange for reckoning,
like his star that rose
and made each one a king.

© Susan Skinner

Candlemas

Celebrating Candlemas

Candlemas is the feast of the purification of the Blessed Virgin Mary, now more popularly called the Presentation of Christ in the Temple, and occurs on 2 February.

The story, in Luke's Gospel, chapter 2, relates how Mary and Joseph took Jesus to the temple when he was 40 days old in accordance with the Jewish law. They made the customary offering of two turtle doves. At the temple they met Simeon and Anna, both of whom were very old. Simeon recognized the Son of God and took Jesus in his arms, thanking God in the words of the Nunc Dimittis.

The practice of blessing and carrying lighted candles round churches began 1,000 years later in Rome and stemmed from a pagan custom of carrying lights round the city to bless it. Christians adopted the symbol of the candle to represent Christ, the light of the world.

If your church has a Candlemas procession, then the children will certainly love to join in although, depending on their ages, it may not be safe for them to carry lights. Here are some safe seasonal activities which can be used in your Sunday school classes.

As a general introduction, read the story from Luke's Gospel. Darken the room as much as possible by closing the curtains. Light one candle and place it in the middle of the room. See how much illumination one small flame gives and how it provides a bright focus in the darkness. This is the effect Jesus has on our souls.

Follow-up for under-fives

Materials
strips of matt white card
stubs of white household candles
yellow powder paint
water
orange crayons
optional materials for making a mobile:
wire coat-hanger
hole-punch
thread or ribbon.

Cut out large candle shapes from the card and write on one side, 'Jesus, light of the world'. The children can colour the flame orange on both sides. On the plain side let them draw 'invisible' patterns with the candle stubs. Wash over the patterns with a weak solution of yellow paint. These could be used as giant bookmarks or pierced, threaded with cotton or ribbon and hung from a coat-hanger to make a seasonal mobile.

Follow-up for older children

Materials

plasticine (or clay, paints and varnish)

household candles

Ask each child to model a candle-holder from the modelling material. If you are using clay, try to provide aprons and remember that handles must be pulled out from the ball of clay rather than stuck on or they will fall off when dry. Place a candle in the holder and use these to illustrate Jesus' story about putting a candle on a stick so that it gives light to all in the house. Clay holders could be painted and varnished in successive weeks and perhaps displayed in church. Extension activities would be to make a pictorial list of all the different forms of light encountered in our daily lives and to consider what it would be like without them. Explain that for Christians, life without Jesus is dark too.

Suitable songs would be 'Jesus, kind above all other' sung to the tune 'Quem Pastores' or used as a prayer (HAMR 456) and 'This little light of mine'(HON 510; JP 258).

© Elizabeth Speight

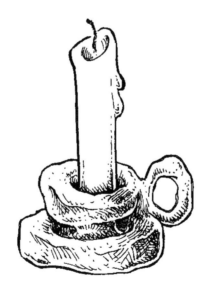

Candlemas all-age service

Maybe we are used to seeing children acting in services for adults. In this teaching service, the adults act to explain the meaning of both Candlemas and baptism to all ages.

Welcome

Hymn 'At the name of Jesus' (HAMNS 148).

Prayer Father, we come together today to worship you,
to listen to what you have to say to us,
to give thanks for what you have done for us,
and to share with you our hopes and needs.
Help us to make good use of our time together,
and when we go to our homes come with us in our hearts,
through Jesus Christ our Lord. Amen

Leader Today it's just 40 days from Christmas, the time when Jesus was born. Today we remember one of the first things in Jesus' life, something that happened not long after he was born. We call it 'The

Presentation of Christ in the Temple', but its more popular name is 'Candlemas'.

In the past, people would come to church at Candlemas and be given a lighted candle to carry in a procession while singing some words from the Bible. This was to remember the day when Jesus was taken to the Jewish temple by his parents for a special ceremony that was always performed after a boy was born.

So the first thing we are going to do is to light this big candle and say together the first Candlemas poems on the sheet.

(*Helper lights candle.*)

All	Light a candle, let its ray tell us of a feast today. Light a candle, let its glow help us find the way to go. Light a candle, let its spark drive out all that's bad and dark. 'Candlemas' we call that day, and it shows us why we say, forty days from Jesus' birth, 'He's a light for all the earth'.
Leader	So Jesus was born 40 days ago. And now Mary and Joseph must take their baby son to the temple in Jerusalem because they have a duty to perform.
Helper	The Lord said to Moses, 'Every first-born male – child or animal – belongs to me.' Moses told the people, 'You must offer every first-born male to the Lord. The animals we must sacrifice, but our sons we shall buy back.'
Joseph	(*Enters with Mary, who carries the baby*) Here we are, Mary my dear. This is the temple gate. I must go and change my money into temple money for the offering. We must give five shekels to God to buy our son back.
Mary	And I must offer two doves – we can't afford a lamb, can we? I'll get them from the Court of the Women and see you back here in a few minutes. (*They exit separately.*)
Leader	So Mary and Joseph are here at the temple with the baby Jesus. Like all new parents they are wondering about the future. They know something special will happen of course because of all the things God told them before Jesus was born, and the things the shepherds said.

(Mary and Joseph return.)

Mary Oh there you are, Joseph. I'm so glad. There's an old man who's been staring at me very strangely. I don't like it. *(Simeon enters from the back)* Look! He's coming towards us now.

Joseph Don't worry, Mary. He looks harmless enough to me. Perhaps he just likes children.

Simeon I can't believe it! At last he is here!

Joseph I'm sorry . . . I don't know what you mean. And who are you?

Simeon My name is Simeon, but that isn't important. Your baby . . . your son . . . he is God's chosen one, the Christ. I have waited so long for this moment. God promised me that I would not die until I had seen the one he would send to save his people. And now here he is! May I hold him?

Mary Well . . . I'm not sure.

Joseph Go on, Mary. You can see what a good man he is. *(Joseph hands baby to Simeon.)*

Simeon *(Holding up the baby and addressing God)*
Thank you, God our Father,
Now I am happy to die.
For I have seen your son,
who is to be the glory of the people of Israel
and a light for the whole world.

Joseph What a wonderful thing to say.

Mary Yes, you make us so happy.

Simeon I'm glad. What I'm telling you is the truth, just as God has shown it to me. *(He hands the baby back)* But be prepared, my dears, for sorrow too. His way will be hard. People will have to decide whether to follow him or not, and he will have many enemies. *(Anna enters)* He will speak the truth, but the truth can divide people as well as set them free.

Anna Excuse me. My name is Anna. I couldn't help hearing what you were saying. I too have been looking for God to do something for his people. Thanks be to him! I must go and tell everyone what has happened.

(All exit.)

Leader	So Mary and Joseph then knew a little more about why Jesus had come. For them it was both good news and bad news. Their child would do wonderful things when he showed the world how much God loves it, just as Simeon had predicted . . . but he would also suffer and die . . . and no parent likes to think of that happening to their child.
	Perhaps you thought Simeon's words sounded a bit familiar. If so that's because we say or sing them at every evening service in church. We are going to sing a version of them now called 'Faithful vigil ended'. As we sing, let's imagine that we are Simeon, glad to find God's promise come true.
Hymn	'Faithful vigil ended' (HAMNS 453).
Leader	But now here are some other parents with their baby. (*Enter Mum with baby, followed by Dad, carrying a baptism candle, and two friends.*) They too have just left a house of God, but in their case it's their local church. Their baby has just been christened – or baptized to give it its proper name.
Mum	(*To the friends*) Thanks, you two, for being godparents.
Dad	Yes, it's good of you.
Friend 1	Oh, think nothing of it. Piece of cake really.
Friend 2	Yes, answer a few questions and that. It wasn't difficult.
Mum	I don't know . . . the vicar came on rather strong about the duties of parents and godparents. 'It's not all over with the christening', he said . . . I hope you took note.
Dad	Ah well, that's his job, isn't it? He's bound to say stuff like that about coming to church and Sunday school. He's drumming up trade, keeping up the collections.
Friend 2	Well what he said about setting her a good example was right, wasn't it? I shall have to try, shan't I?
Friend 1	But he went on a bit about teaching her the Christian faith. I mean, how are we supposed to do that? That's his job.
Mum	But I think he's right. She's bound to grow up like us, isn't she? We're her parents and her friends, so she'll learn most things from us.
Dad	What was all that about putting the cross on her forehead in water . . . 'To show that she belongs to Jesus', he said.
Friend 2	That just means she's a member of the Church.

Friend 1	I liked the bit where he gave her a lighted candle. Look it says on it: 'Shine as a light in the world'.
Mum	I hope she will.
Dad	Anyway, she's properly done now. Let's get on with the party!
Mum	Well, I hope you're all going to take it a bit more seriously. I want our child to grow up honest and good. I want her to be a 'light in the world' . . . and you're all supposed to help her! (*Stamps foot and exits angrily.*)
Friend 1	Oh dear, I hope we haven't upset her.
Dad	No, don't worry. She takes things too seriously sometimes.
Friend 2	Yes, it's only a christening after all!
	(*All exit.*)
Leader	'Only a christening' indeed! Baptism means much more than that. Mum had the right idea. When we were baptized we too were signed with the cross in water on our foreheads to show that we belong to Jesus. We too are meant to shine as lights in the world like Simeon said Jesus would. Later on, Jesus talked about himself as a light too.
Helper	Jesus said: 'I am the light of the world. Whoever follows me will have the light of life and will never walk in darkness.'
Leader	So let's just think for a minute or two about the kinds of light and darkness that Jesus meant. (*Have two columns on a board: 'Light' and 'Darkness'.*) What sort of things should we put in the 'Light' column? (*Good things like goodness, kindness, peace, love, sharing, happiness.*) And what sort of things in the 'Darkness' column? (*Bad things like evil, hurt, war, hate, selfishness, sadness.*)
	So Jesus came to show us, and teach us about, all these good things and to destroy the things of darkness. That's why he called himself the light of the world, and that's why we celebrate Candlemas, remembering the time when his light was first seen and recognized by other people.
	So the light of Jesus is meant to be passed on and shared. We can show that by lighting a small candle from this big candle and saying together the second Candlemas poem.
	(*Helper lights small candle from large one.*)
All	Light a candle, let its ray make a feast of every day.

Light a candle, let its glow
show us all the way to go.
Light a candle, let its spark
drive from us what's bad and dark.
'Candlemas' we call this day
because it shows us why we say,
'Jesus' light is what we need,
we will follow where he leads'.

Song   'From the darkness came light' (*Come and Praise*, BBC, 1978).

Leader   We're going to pray the prayer on the sheet. Let's keep our eyes open to see the big candle – the Jesus candle – and the little candle by the side of it, which is meant to be us.

Jesus – any light, any goodness, that we have comes from you.

All   Shine on us, shine in us.

Leader   Jesus, the world needs your light now more than ever.

All   Shine on us, shine in us.

Leader   Jesus, thank you for being the light that shows us the way we should go, and helps us see life's dangers.

All   Shine on us, shine in us.

Leader   Jesus, help us to grow in all that is right and good and true.

All   Shine on us, shine in us.

Leader   Jesus, we pray for all those places where darkness seems to be in control.

All   Shine on us, shine in us.

Leader   Jesus, we confess that we have not always walked in your light. We have done wrong and gone wrong and been a bad example to others. We ask your forgiveness.

All   Shine on us, shine in us.

Leader   So help us to grow in all that is good and true until we shine with your light. Amen.

**Offertory
Hymn**   'Christ is the world's true light' (HAMNS 346).

Blessing

© Don Tordoff

Mothering Sunday

Activities for Mothering Sunday

Mothering Sunday is a time to thank God for our mothers and those who have cared for us, and for their love in expressing his love for us. Children mostly come to know the love of God for them through the care and concern of those who bring them up. These craft activities are in the form of thank-you gifts to be given to a mother or carer. Begin the activities for all ages by re-telling the story from Mark 10.13-16 of people bringing children to Jesus.

With the under-fives: Leading by the hand poster

Materials
1 sheet white A4 paper
coloured A4 paper
crayons
gummed paper shapes
black felt-tip pen

Before the session draw round an adult hand on the white paper. Using a ruler draw a 5-cm border round the edge of the paper with a black felt-tip pen. Write on the words, 'Thank you for leading me by the hand', or 'Thank you for leading me by the hand and showing me Jesus'. Photocopy as many copies of this as you need for your children on the coloured paper.

Explain to the children that the hand on the sheet of paper is the hand of the person who takes them by the hand across the road, who puts them to bed, who puts food in their hands, who leads them to playgroup and church, and who helps them pray and praise Jesus. This can be the hand of one or many people, but mainly their mums. Tell the children that today we are thanking Jesus for the way our mums lead us to him. Ask the children to put their own hand inside the adult one and draw round it. Encourage the children to colour in their hand and to stick gummed paper shapes around the border.

With the five to nines: A Bible bookmark

Materials
photocopy the bookmark on pieces of card, with ribbon hole punched in
pencils, crayons or felt-tips
glue
sequins, stars and glitter
thin ribbon to tie on

Ask the children how they came to know Jesus. Talk about the people that have helped and particularly their mothers. Is there anything they have discovered about God the Father, Jesus or the Holy Spirit this year which they could tell their mothers?

Encourage the children to write on the back of the bookmark something that they have discovered about God recently. Then they can colour in the lettering and picture on the bookmark, and decorate it with sequins, stars and glitter. Give them a short length of thin ribbon to tie on the bottom.

Alternatively, the children could design their own bookmark with 'Thank you for loving me' on it.

With the over-tens: A gift-filled home

Materials
photocopy and enlarge the house template on pieces of card

scissors

glue sticks

pencils and crayons

Discuss with the children the ups and downs of home life and what makes a house or flat a home. Talk about some of the ways mothers help them to get to know God at home, like Bible reading, praying with them, saying grace before meals, having a special Sunday lunch, and celebrations at festival times. Suggest that the children make the templates into their own homes by drawing windows and doors and drawing members of their family on the outside or looking through the windows. Use the box template on p. 64. (A finished version of the house is also shown on p. 61.)

On the roof they can write a special thank-you message to their mothers or carers for their homes. Inside they can put a tiny gift of their choice.

© Jean Thomson

63

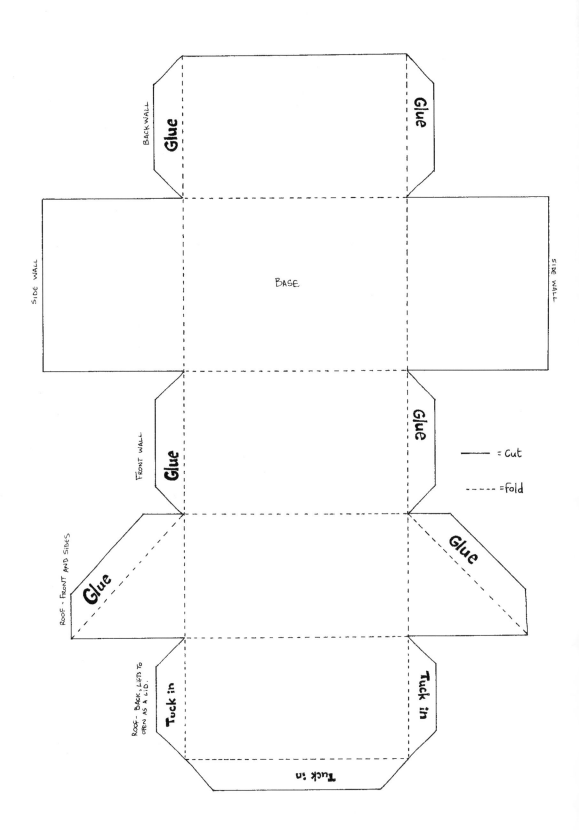

BACK WALL

Glue

Glue

SIDE WALL

SIDE WALL

BASE

FRONT WALL

Glue

Glue

ROOF - FRONT AND SIDES

Glue

Glue

ROOF - BACK, LIFTS TO OPEN AS A LID.

Tuck in

Tuck in

Tuck in

──────── = Cut

- - - - - - = Fold

Ta Ma or soft soap – A myth retold

This sketch for Mothering Sunday requires only one actor but plenty of practice, in order to co-ordinate the actions and the props at the correct time. Ta Ma *or* soft soap *light-heartedly looks at the idea of the 'Supermum', using the language and brand names of well-known commercials.*

Cast
Narrator
Props Manager
Supermum

Props
baby bottle (bb), saucepan (sp), whistle (wh), chauffeur's cap (cc), dustpan and brush (d&p), washing powder (wp), telephone (te), shopping bag (sb), book (bo), first-aid box (fab), lawn mower (lm)

As the activity connected with each item is mentioned in the story, the Props Manager hands it to, or removes it from, Supermum

Narrator We present a day in the life of Supermum, who really is a marvel. (*Enter Supermum.*)

At 7.00 am, Supermum wakes up singing and starts her new day. First she feeds baby (*bb*) with Nestlés baby milk, then cooks (*sp*) breakfast: Weetabix for the children, Special K for her husband, followed by Del Monte Orange, and Danish bacon and Typhoo tea. She referees (*wh*) a quarrel between the two older children so that her husband can read his newspaper undisturbed, finds his car keys and (*cc*) drives her husband to the station, drops her two older children off to school and returns home.

Then she settles down to cleaning (*d & b*) the entire house with a smile on her face as she is using an Addis broom, new Flash and an

Electrolux vacuum cleaner. In between she answers (*te*) five tele-phone calls, (three wrong numbers and two double-glazing salesmen), deals with a screaming baby (*bo*) and (*wp*) a day's washing (Persil washes whiter and it shows), writes her shopping list (*sb*), feeds baby again (*bb*) and drives off (*cc* and *sb*) to Sainsbury's for the shopping. Here she whizzes around the super-market buying wholesome, nutritious, non-fattening and additive-free food for the entire family, and still has change from a £10 note. Unruffled by the baby's screaming she administers first aid when he traps his fingers in the car door (*fab*), drives back home singing nursery rhymes and unloads the shopping.

Then she answers the telephone again while feeding the baby (*te* and *bb*), cooks herself (*sp*) a low-calorie lunch. She decides she hasn't got time to re-decorate the front room, so instead she mows the front lawn (*lm*) and cleans the car (*cc* and *d&p*) while the baby is asleep. She then answers the telephone (*te*) (her mother) and the baby awakes screaming (*bb* then *bo* then *fab* then *d&p*). It's now time (drops *bb, bo, fab* and *d&p*) to collect (*cc*) her two children from school.

When they return she prepares their tea (*sp*), referees two squab-bles, (*wh* and *te*) while answering an involved telephone call from her mother-in-law over the respective merits of dried and tinned prunes. When baby screams again (*bb* and *bo*), having failed to get satisfaction from Dr Spock, she applies him to the child's seat of learning and it stops.

She washes the older children (*wp*) and reads them a story (*bo*) and puts them to bed. She starts to cook (*sp*) her husband a delicious soufflé when the telephone rings (*te*) waking up the eldest child who is immediately sick (*wp* and *fab*). The soufflé burns (*sp*) and her husband walks in saying: 'Have you had a good day, darling?' Supermum sweetly replies, 'About average, my dear.'

© Donald Dowling

Easter

Surprise, surprise
An all-age Easter service

The emphasis here is upon the surprise of Easter and how the resurrection story urges us to remember that we are God's surprises to each other, just as Jesus was God's great surprise to us. There are a number of parts of the service that demand careful preparation by groups of people well in advance.

Welcome and introductory sentence Luke 24.1

Hymn   'The Day of Resurrection' (HAMNS 75; HON 474).

Talk   *The talk is divided into several sections throughout the service. It is important to be sure of what to talk about at each stage so that the service flows well.*

What a wonderful surprise the disciples had!

What is a surprise? *Ask everyone this question, and elicit an answer which defines it as something good . . . unexpected . . . that brightens up your day . . . that brings joy.*

Reading   Matthew 28.1–10 or Mark 16.1–8

Perhaps younger members of the congregation could show others the Easter Garden, or a picture of the resurrection which they have prepared earlier, to illustrate the account.

Talk   How amazed they all must have been . . . they thought that their best friend and only hope was dead. Yet here he was alive again . . . something so good, so unexpected, that brought them so much joy, made their day, and brightened up their lives. The best surprise of all.

After they saw Jesus alive again, many of his friends were so joyful because they realized that God's love is stronger than death. They wanted to tell everyone about it. Jesus knew they could do it because that's exactly what God has made us all for: to show everybody that God is full of surprises, the surprise of ourselves and even more importantly, the surprise of the resurrection.

Hymn   'Thine be the glory, risen conquering Son' (HAMNS 428; MP 689).

Have some brightly coloured brighten-up-the-day sunshines made from card for the younger children to hold up during the next part.

Having primed them, invite four or five people of different ages, such as a mum and baby, a child, a teenager and two older people to come up to the front. Tell everyone that here we have examples of some of the millions of God's surprises. Have fun asking what it is about them which brightens up our day. Keep it simple, encourage suggestions such as a welcoming smile, enthusiasm, trust, humour, and so on. With each suggestion of what it is about these people that brightens up our day, children in the congregation could be encouraged to hold up their sunshines.

It might come as a surprise to us that we are all God's surprises, and surprises have work to do. Listen to the next reading.

Reading   Colossians 3.1–11, or just verses 1 and 8–10

Song   'This little light of mine', HON 510; JP 258).

Talk   It is important to remember that we are each made especially by God for each other, to be lights in the world, to enjoy each other and to learn from each other, and it starts with simple things. (*Maybe the sunshines could be held up again when the following examples are given.*) Simple things such as kind words, honesty, patience, truth, enthusiasm and trust. (*Maybe ask for help from the congregation to link with what was said about the people at the front earlier on.*) Sometimes it is hard work to be the surprises God wants us to be, but the more we do it the more we will see God's surprises in other people.

Sometimes it is easy to spoil the surprise. (*Again ask for help here, and perhaps ask the children to cover their sunshines with their hands, like clouds, when giving examples.*) We can spoil the surprise by saying something unkind, thinking the worst, lying and so on. The more we do that, the less we see God's surprises in other people, so that life is unhappy and dull.

The story of the resurrection tells us that if we can trust God we will see more and more of his surprises, and more of the joy and brightness of his love. (*Ask the children to hold up their sunshines and invite everyone to shout 'alleluia' as loud as they can.*)

Offertory hymn 'Father I place into your hands' (HON 121; JP 42).

Intercessions Based on the format from *The Alternative Service Book 1980*, p. 125.

Before the service, you need to ask groups of people of different ages to come together to produce short prayers in the following way:

One group looks at national/diocesan/deanery church papers and produces a short prayer celebrating God's surprises and asking forgiveness where surprises have been 'spoilt' in the life of the local, national and world-wide church.

Another group looks at national and local papers and produces a short prayer celebrating God's surprises and asking forgiveness where surprises have been spoilt in the locality and wider world.

A third group looks at a community news-letter or parish magazine to produce a prayer for families, friends and the local community.

A fourth group, in praying for the sick, may focus on the difficulty of seeing God's surprises when life is hard because of illness and sadness, and the importance of the glimpses of God shown by our love and care.

Those who remember the dead may rejoice that those who have died are enjoying the fullness of God's surprises. May God help us not to be frightened of such a full and happy life.

If younger children are involved in producing prayers, they might like to present them in the form of a picture, perhaps with a few simple words.

Final hymn 'Majesty' (HON 327; MP 454).

The blessing

© Judith Sadler

An Easter service for young children

Materials
Easter garden
paschal candle
individual candles
sand tray or pricket stand

This service begins at the Easter garden. Place a rug on the floor for everyone to sit on.

Hymn   (*Use an appropriate Easter hymn that is familiar to the children.*)

Leader   Lord, we come to praise you for the glorious resurrection of Jesus at Easter. Give us joy and devotion to you as we offer you our prayers and praises.

All gather around the Easter garden and talk about what can be seen there.

Reading

It was now early on Sunday morning and it was still dark, Mary from Magdala came along to the tomb. She looked at it – someone had taken the stone away and it was open. She ran off to Peter and the friend whom Jesus had loved dearly.

'The master's been taken from the tomb,' she said, 'and we don't know where he's been put.'

Peter and the other friend of Jesus ran together to the tomb. The other friend got to it first; he could run faster than Peter. He peered into the tomb – the linen cloths were lying there alright – but he stayed outside. Peter came up after him and went straight inside. He gazed at the sheets lying there and at the head cloth, rolled up by itself away from the sheets. The other friend now came in and saw it all. Mary's story was true.

(From Alan Dale, *New World*, Oxford University Press, 1967.)

Move over as a group to the Paschal candle and sing a hymn such as 'This little light of mine' 'Shine, Jesus, shine' *or* 'Colours of day' (HON 510, 317, 87).

Reading

The day passed, and it was now late in the evening. The friends of Jesus were together in the house. They were frightened of the Jewish leaders, so they had locked the doors. Then – there was Jesus standing among them.

'Peace be with you,' he said. With these words, he let them see his hands and his side. They saw it was Jesus and they were overjoyed.

(From Alan Dale, *New World*, Oxford University Press, 1967.)

Show the children the Paschal candle and light a candle for each child from it. Obviously this must be done with great care, and each child supervised by the adult with whom they came. As soon as they have their candle, the children move to the sand tray / pricket stand and place the candle there. The tray / stand should be a little way from the Paschal candle, perhaps in another part of the church such as a side chapel.

Leader   Lord God, we thank you for making Jesus' friends very happy because they knew that he was with them. Please help us to be good and happy friends of Jesus too. Amen.

The Lord's Prayer

End the service with a final hymn and the blessing or grace.

© Michael Camp

The Easter Bunny Show

TV game shows have become the staple diet of many people's lives. This sketch is a humorous parody of these, at the same time providing a telling message about Easter. It is particularly suitable for older children or all-age events.

Voice   (*Over microphone, in over-the-top style*) Ladies and gentlemen, boys and girls, welcome to today's edition of the Easter Bunny Show. Please put your hands together and give an enormous Easter Bunny welcome to your host, Roger Rabbitt. (*Music.*)

(*Roger is a typical game-show host, very slick, keen on catch phrases, etc.*)

Roger   Nice to see you – nice to see you! Well, it's good to be back again on this special Easter Bunny Show. Are you having a good time there kids? I bet you are. Any of you fancy coming up here to help me? Well, that's tough because I don't need any help today because I've got my lovely assistant waiting back stage. So, let's give a great big bunny kind of a round of applause for the Easter Bunny.

(*Music. Applause, but nothing happens*) I guess that little bunny must be a little shy. Let's try one more round of applause shall we? Come on, let's see how much noise we can make for the Easter Bunny. (*Music. Applause, but still nothing. Roger looks perplexed.*) Well, I wonder what's up with our bunny today. (*Moves up stage and calls off*) Oh Easter Bunny – where are you?

(*Bunny is not keen to come out at first because of his costume! However, with the offer of money he comes out reluctantly and plays the part of the pretty assistant, although his words are not always what Roger is expecting. As the show goes on, however, Bunny gets more and more into it and begins to play the part with more conviction and gusto.)*

Bunny   (*Off*) I'm not doing it!

Roger   What?

Bunny   (*Off*) I said I'm not doing it!

Roger   Oh come on, Easter Bunny. Don't be shy. Come on out.

Bunny   (*Off*) No. Get someone else.

Roger   There isn't anyone else. Anyway, everyone's waiting and you wouldn't want to disappoint all these lovely children now would you? (*Smiles to audience*) (*Hisses to Bunny*) I'll pay you double.

Bunny   (*Off-reluctantly*) Oh, all right then.

Roger   So let's hear it one more time for the Easter Bunny. (*Music.*)

              (*Bunny comes out. It is a man – suitably attired!*)

Bunny   (*Through his smile he hisses to Roger as he comes on*) Next time your assistant falls ill, find someone else!

Roger   So let's not waste any more time and get straight on with our first game. And what is our first game Easter Bunny?

Bunny   Well Roger, the first game tonight is called 'What's in the box?'

Roger   What's in the box? Sounds good. And why is it called that?

Bunny   (*Smiling sweetly*) I have no idea Roger.

Roger   (*Taken by surprise for a moment*) Ah well, I guess it's called that because we get to see what's in the box! So, Easter Bunny, who's our first special fluffy Easter chick of a contestant this morning?

Bunny   How should I know, Roger!

Roger   Well, Easter Bunny, perhaps you'd like to fetch him anyway.

              (*Bunny fetches the first contestant, Derek. In some vague way he is dressed up to represent an Easter chick. Derek is not at all bright, although he should not be made to sound stupid.) So let's have another great big Easter Bunny kind of round of applause for our first contestant. (Music. Derek enters.) Welcome, welcome, welcome. Nice to see you – nice to see you! And you are?*

Derek   (*Slightly surprised – he isn't very bright!*) I'm the first contestant!

Roger	And your name is?
Derek	Derek.
Roger	Derek! What a lovely name. Do you mind if I call you Dirk, Derek?
Derek	Er, well, yes I do, actually.
Roger	So, Dirk, tell the audience, where have you come from today?
Derek	Er, just back there behind the screens.
Roger	You feeling nervous, Dirk?
Derek	No, not really.
Roger	Well, don't be. Easter Bunny here will look after you, won't you Bunnykins? (*Bunny is about to voice his reluctance but Roger has moved on already.*) So, Bunnykins, bring on our second contestant (*Music. Bunny and contestant 2, Shirley, come on.*) So, Bunnydrops, tell us all about our second contestant.
Bunny	This is Shirley from Shaftesbury and she's sure she's sharp enough to play today's game of 'What's in the Box?' (*Music.*)
Roger	So Shirley, are you feeling confident?
Shirley	Oh yes, Roger.
Roger	And why's that Shirley?
Shirley	Because I've already met Derek back stage.
Roger	Fair point. So all we need now is the box. Bunny, why don't you go and fetch the box while I explain the rules?
Bunny	Fetch it yourself! (*Roger shrugs and goes, leaving Bunny to explain.*) So Dirk and Shirley, are you ready to play? (*They nod vigorously.*) Today's game is very simple. (*Roger appears with the box which he places by Bunny.*) In the box are four objects which all have some connection with Easter. All you have to do is to tell us what that connection is.
Roger	So let's play 'What's in the box?' (*Music.*) Anyone out there in the audience want to guess what our first object might be? (*Listens for a moment.*) Did I hear someone say an Easter egg? Well Easter Bunny, are there any eggs in the box?
Bunny	I don't know Roger. Let's see shall we? (*Produces eggs one at a time – throws first to Roger.*) One egg.
Roger	Er, thank you Easter Bunny.

Bunny	Two eggs. (*Again throws to Roger.*)
Roger	Er, thank you again.
Bunny	Three eggs. (*Goes to throw it.*)
Roger	(*Who has hands full*) No, no, no Bunny! (*Bunny is getting his own back and throws it anyway. Fortunately Roger can juggle!*) So Shirley, tell us, what's the connection between eggs and Easter?
Shirley	Eggs represent new life because Jesus brought us the chance to have new life by dying for us.
Roger	That's a good answer Shirley, but it's not what I have here on the card. Derek, can you take it for a bonus?
Derek	Er, is it because Easter eggs are made of chocolate . . . and kids like chocolate . . . so we have them at Easter?
Roger	Is the correct answer. Well done Dirk (*Tosses the eggs into the audience – they are, of course, hard boiled.*) So let's see what else is in the box. Any ideas from the audience? Well, let's see shall we? Easter Bunny, tell us, what's in the box? (*Music.*)
Bunny	(*Reaches in and pulls out a cross*) It's a cross. So Shirley, can you make a connection between a cross and Easter?
Shirley	Well, that's easy. Jesus was crucified on a cross. It's a symbol for the sacrifice that Jesus made on our behalf.
Roger	No, I'm sorry – can you take it Dirk?
Derek	Is it because you find a cross on top of a hot-cross bun?
Roger	Right again. Well Dirk, you're certainly on top form tonight. I wonder what we'll find in the box next. Come on, Shirley, don't give up. There's still plenty of time to win. So let's see, what's in the box? (*Music.*) (*This time Roger himself reaches in and produces a rubber chicken*) It's a chicken. (*He's nonplussed.*)
Bunny	Here, how did that get in there? That's my lunch. (*Grabs hold of it.*)
Roger	Ah, bit of a surprise item there. Well, moving right on. Easter Bunny tell us, what's in the box? (*Music.*)
Bunny	Well, Roger, it's a rock.
Roger	A bit tricky this one. Any ideas Dirk?
Derek	No, not really.
Roger	No surprise there then. Shirley?

Shirley	Well, Easter Bunny, the rock makes me think of the stone which was rolled away from Jesus' tomb when he came back to life – and that's why we celebrate Easter Day.
Roger	Really, you mean it's not just about chocolate and bunnies and fluffy Easter chicks?
Derek	Oh come on Roger, even I know that one!
Roger	(*Trying to move on*) So Easter Bunny, is there anything else in the box?
Bunny	(*Looks in*) No Roger, the box is empty.
Derek	(*Suddenly coming to life*) Which represents the empty tomb.

Roger & Bunny (*Taken aback*) What?

Derek	The empty tomb – Jesus rose from the dead and so the tomb was empty.
Shirley	And that's why we celebrate Easter Day.
	(*Roger and Bunny go to interrupt but they are bundled out of the way.*)
Derek	(*Becoming like Roger*) Well, that's all for today, so thank you for watching – and don't forget – when you're tucking into your Easter eggs, ask yourself, 'What's in the tomb?' (*Music.*)
Shirley	Nothing.
Derek	That's right, Shirley. You won't find Jesus in the tomb because . . .
All	(*Big finish*) Jesus is alive!
	(*Closing music. All bow and exit.*)

© Tim Wheeler

Early one morning

Cast

The Chief Priest, Levi and two guards: Sam and Ben

(The chief priest is sleeping. Suddenly there is loud, insistent knocking.)

Chief   What's that? Who's there? Who's disturbing the chief priest at this unearthly hour?

Levi   *(Calling in panic)* Your grace! Your worship! Your very reverend!

Chief   Levi, it's you! What's the matter?

Levi   Oh sir, something terrible has happened. It's awful! Panic, panic!

Chief   Now calm down and tell me.

Levi   The Galilean that was executed on Friday . . .

Chief   Yes, Jesus bar-Joseph, I know, go on.

Levi   The tomb, the tomb . . .

Chief   Yes, Joseph's tomb, where Governor Pilate allowed them to put the body.

Levi   The stone, the stone . . .

Chief   Yes, the large stone that was rolled in front and the temple seal put on it.

Levi   The guards, the guards . . .

Chief   Yes, the two temple guards Governor Pilate allowed us to post at the tomb.

Levi   Gone! Disappeared! Vanished!

Chief   The guards?

Levi   No, no . . . gone!

Chief   The stone?

Levi   No, no . . . gone!

Chief   The body?

Levi   Yes – the body. Gone, disappeared, vanished!

Chief   (*Furious*) WHAT! The very thing we wanted to prevent.

Levi   Yes, yes! Disappeared, gone without trace.

Chief   (*Seething*) Are the guards still there?

Levi   Yes, in a state of utter terror and confusion.

Chief   I'll utterly terrorize and confuse them! Fetch them here – now!

Levi   Yes, I'll go.

Chief   We'll make an example of them.

Levi   Yes, an example.

Chief   Execute them.

Levi   Yes, execute them.

Chief   In public.

Levi   Yes, in public.

Chief   And I'll see they lose their pension! What are you doing here? Fetch them now!

Levi	Yes, your grace. (*Exits.*)
Chief	The very thing we wanted to avoid was his followers coming to steal the body – and now this. (*Sits with head in hands.*)
	(*Levi goes to the two guards at the back of the church or hall.*)
Levi	Sergeant Sam and Corporal Ben, you are to report to the chief priest immediately!
Sam	Very well, sir. (*They set off up the aisle or gangway.*)
Ben	Oh, this ain't so good.
Sam	We'll be in right trouble.
Ben	Wish I'd never said I'd do this extra duty.
Sam	Well I needed the money – a good bit of overtime, 10 shekels an hour.
Ben	What do you need extra money for?
Sam	Promised the family a trip to Palestine-Disney, didn't I?
Ben	I'm saving up for one of those new four-by-four off-road chariots.
Sam	We'll be lucky to get anything now – probably end up in jail.
Ben	If we do we'll miss the big match. Jerusalem United against Jericho North End.
Sam	The finals of the milk-and-honey cup.
Ben	What are we going to tell the chief priest happened this morning?
Sam	Tell him the truth.
Ben	He'll never believe that – nobody will.
Sam	He's going to have to try.
	(*They arrive at the chief priest's house as Levi catches up with them.*)
Levi	Come on, smarten yourselves up a bit, the chief priest wants to see you immediately. (*Announces*) The temple guards, sir.
Chief	You fools, you incompetent fools! Blind drunk, asleep on duty, and you let his followers come and steal the body.
Sam & Ben	But, but . . .
Chief	You've got it coming to you for this. Just what we didn't want to happen – just what you were there to prevent.
Sam	But it wasn't like that at all.

Ben   We weren't drunk and we weren't asleep.

Sam   Nobody came and stole the body.

Chief   You'd better have a good story to explain this.

Sam   We have.

Ben   But you're not going to believe it.

Chief   You're dead right I'm not, but you might as well tell me.

(*They dramatically relive the events at the tomb.*)

Sam   It wasn't so bad during the day. We took it in turns to sleep, we reckoned there was no danger.

Ben   The tomb was still secure as it went dark last night.

Sam   It was clear, lots of stars, very cold. Very quiet in the garden.

Ben   You felt you had to talk in whispers. Just before dawn we were cold, but wide awake – and sober.

Sam   There was a strange, eerie light. The ground trembled . . .

Ben   The stone rocked in its groove and the seal snapped off . . .

Sam   I heard a roaring in my ears, my limbs shook and I was filled with a conviction – I must look in the tomb.

Ben   We heaved the stone to one side and looked in . . .

Sam   That strange light filled the cave . . .

Ben   The tomb was empty . . .

Sam   Just a faint smell of incense . . .

Ben   And a bitter smell . . . of myrrh.

Sam   Everything was quiet and peaceful once more.

Chief   (*After a pause*) That's impossible . . . unbelievable. Rubbish! We can't have a story like this getting about! We must seal up the tomb before anyone sees it. Levi, off you go.

Levi   I'm afraid it's already too late. As I came away after these two I saw some women, his followers I think, coming into the garden through the side gate.

Chief   Never mind – nobody's going to believe all this. You two – you are to spread it about that the Galilean's followers came last night and stole the body.

Sam & Ben   But sir . . .

Chief   We'll double your pay for last night's shift – and I'll add a special bonus to cover the damage to your reputation.

Sam   Well, in that case . . .

Ben   I think we could agree.

Levi   You might as well. Nobody will believe what you've just told us.

Chief   Good. Well, I'm glad that's sorted out. A couple of days and this will all be forgotten about and nobody will ever hear again of this Jesus. (*Turns away*.)

Sam   (*To Ben*) Funny thing, Ben. I feel there's more to it.

Ben   Me too. We'll have to wait and see.

© John Cooper

The boy who saw Easter

This companion story to The girl who saw Christmas *is a chance for children to imagine themselves inside the events of Easter morning.*

Matthew was sleeping soundly when the pet lamb by his side woke him.

'Baaa,' it bleated, nuzzling his neck.

'Ssh! Don't wake the others,' whispered Matthew, yawning and throwing off his goatskin blanket at the same time.

Inside the small, one-roomed house, his father, mother and younger sister were lying asleep under their goatskins. They did not stir. Matthew got up, splashed water from the stone water-jar onto his face and led the lamb outside. It cropped happily at the grass by the roadside.

Daylight was breaking over the Judaean hills. The last stars were fading in the yellow streaks of sunlight over Jerusalem. The Sabbath was over. Soon Matthew's father would walk to the city to work. His mother and sister would collect water from the well, bake the bread and do the household chores. And he would lead their herd of goats to graze on the hillside.

He was glad he had woken early. There was something he wanted to do on this first day of the week. He wanted to find out where the holy carpenter had been buried. He had been crucified on the Friday, three days before.

Matthew had met him in the village earlier that year when he had been passing through with his disciples. He had healed lame John who had been a cripple from birth, and had told everyone wonderful stories about God. He had even drunk water from *their* family drinking bowl. Later though, things had gone wrong. Cruel men had told lies about him and had got the Roman governor, Pontius Pilate, to order his execution. Matthew had felt very unhappy that Friday, but he knew he would be less sad if he could find out where the body lay.

He ran steadily along the road to Jerusalem which was about a kilometre and a half away. There weren't many people about so early in the morning, but ahead of him as he turned a bend, strode a young woman carrying a jar of ointment and some spices in a leather bag. He could smell the spices as he came up behind her and knew by the shape of the jar what it contained. Looking at the red curly hair that escaped from her veil, he recognized her. She was Mary Magdalene, a friend of the carpenter. Surely she must know where he was buried. He wouldn't speak to her, though. He knew grown-ups. They often made excuses if a boy asked a question they didn't want to answer. He would follow her and see where she went.

He took great care not to be seen in case she might think that he was a look-out boy for the robbers who hid among the rocks on the mountainside. Or even that he was a thief himself. Once he threw himself down in a nearby ditch when she looked back and another time he crouched behind a gnarled old olive tree. Nearing the great city more travellers joined them, taking in produce to sell in the market or going to work in the shops and great houses there.

He was right behind Mary as they passed through the city gate.

'Get out of the way!' yelled a man driving a heavily laden cart pulled by a donkey. It rumbled through to the countryside and Matthew had to squeeze into a nearby doorway to avoid being run over.

Next a Roman centurion, mounted on a white horse, trotted down the narrow street followed by six of his foot-soldiers. Matthew had to stop once more. In the noise and bustle of people moving about in this great city he found that he had lost sight of Mary Magdalene. Tears of disappointment filled his eyes as he realized he couldn't find her in the narrow alleys. He had to find her. Then he had to get back before he was missed or his father would whip him. What was he to do? He hated the noise and the crowds, and especially the smell. The city was not sweet like the hillside. Just as he was about to turn for home, he saw the garden.

It was cool under the shade of the trees. He slipped in through the gate. Maybe he could rest and think what to do there. He found himself walking down a sandy path which twisted and turned and before long he could see the city wall once more before him. Soon, right in front of him was a tomb built in the rock. What was strange, though, was that the huge round stone that stopped up the entrance had been rolled away. Who would have done that so early in the morning? It would need several men working together.

As Matthew puzzled over it, he saw her, Mary Magdalene. She had placed her jar of ointment and the package of spices by the dark entrance and was bending her head low to look inside. He crept closer. She was talking to someone unseen. There was a brightness at the back of the cavern above the shelf on which the body should have lain. But there was no body there, just a glimpse of two creatures with wings.

Matthew was very frightened, and he ran a little way back down the path. Yet he *had* to know what it was all about. He hid behind an olive tree, the feel of its familiar, rough bark comforting him. When he turned to look again at the tomb he saw Mary facing a tall, bearded man dressed in the long white robe of a rabbi. She was saying urgently, 'If you are the gardener, tell me where he has been laid and I'll take him away.'

Although he could not see the whole of his face, the stranger did not look like a gardener to Matthew. He was trying to remember if he had seen him before when the man uttered one word: 'Mary.'

Immediately, Mary fell at his feet and cried out, 'Master!'

She would have seized hold of his robe, but he said, 'Do not touch me. I have not yet ascended to the Father. But go, tell my brothers that I am returning to the Father, to my God and your God.'

Matthew felt a wonderful happiness in his heart as though he had been given the best present ever, for the man had stepped back and now Matthew could see his face. It was his friend, the holy carpenter, Jesus. In some strange way he was not dead but alive. Matthew wanted to run forward to meet him, but Mary Magdalene came flying down the path and almost knocked him over. When he looked again, Jesus was not there.

Matthew knew that he had to get home and tell his family what had happened — that he had seen Jesus alive. Whether they would believe his story he didn't know, but he just had to tell them. Like Mary, he flew back down the path that first Easter morning, his eyes shining and his face full of glory.

© Sheila Forsdyke

Footprints

All-age services for the Easter weekend

The theme for the Easter weekend is footprints; those we can imagine going to and from the cross, and then to and from the empty tomb. The theme develops over the weekend.

1. Good Friday activity morning

Introduction

This is in many ways a sad time, because we remember that Jesus died on the cross. But it is also Good Friday, because that death showed us how much Jesus loves us, and also because it was not the end of the story. We look forward to Easter Day when we remember Jesus coming back alive.

Activity suggestions

a)   Making name badges in the shape of a cross.

b)   Decorating cross-shaped biscuits.

c)   Decorating eggs and making Easter gifts to take home.

2. Good Friday all-age service

(to finish the activity morning)

Leader   While you have been doing your activities, I have been doing mine. I have laid this trail of footprints (*made of paper*) up to the cross. If you look carefully, you will see that they stop there, and then turn and come away. People came to see Jesus on the cross. They had all sorts of different thoughts in their minds as they did so. Some came because they loved him. Some because they hated him. We have come because we love him and want to know more about how much he loves us.

Prayer   Short prayer thanking God for Good Friday.

Song   'We are marching in the light of God' ('Siyahamba' – WP 135).

Leader   How do we know we can march in the light of God? Because we know God loves us. We know God loves us because of the cross. You've been making crosses out of biscuits this morning. There are lots of other crosses in church as well. Look at one of them as we sing:

Song   'Beneath the Cross of Jesus' (SF 39).

Leader   The first of the crosses you made today is very special. I have one too. What is special about it? It has your name on it. Mine has my name. This shows us that Jesus loves *each one of us*. He doesn't just love everyone in a general sort of way. He loves *you* and he loves *me*. Just like the next song says:

Song   'I'm special' (JP 106).

Leader   In our last song we will sing that we are 'walking in faith and victory'. The footsteps coming away from the cross aren't very victorious. But when we come to church on Sunday we'll look at them again. We will then see how these words became true of Jesus' friends, and how they can become true for us.

Song   'Be bold' (JP 14).

Blessing

3. Good Friday one hour's devotion: footsteps to and from the cross

Leader (*Tell everyone about the activity morning and the footsteps.*) During the coming hour there will be the chance to meditate on some of those who made the journey to the cross – but with the first hymn we'll go back to the journey into Jerusalem, when many happy footprints were made.

Song 'All glory, laud and honour' (HAMNS 328).

Meditation Mark 14.66–72. No footsteps for Peter.

Mark 15.1,11–32a. Footsteps for the priests.

Song 'It is a thing most wonderful' (HAMNS 70).

Meditation Luke 23.26–31. Footsteps for women of Jerusalem.

Luke 23.32–49. Footsteps for the thief and the centurion.

Song 'When I survey the wondrous cross' (HAMNS 67).

Meditation John 19.25–30. Footsteps for Mary and John.

Song 'There is a green hill' (HAMNS 137).

Meditation 1 Peter 2.21–25. Peter got there in the end.

4. Easter morning all-age service

(Rearrange the paper footprints so that two tracks now go up the aisle of the church to an Easter garden at the front on one side. The acting can be done by volunteers. Tell them what to do as you go, and walk with them. No rehearsal is needed.)

Hymn 'Jesus Christ is risen today' (HAMNS 77).

Prayer Use one of the introductory prayers from *Patterns for Worship* such as:

Lord, direct our thoughts
teach us to pray,
lift up our hearts to worship you
in Spirit and in truth,
through Jesus Christ. Amen.

(*Patterns for Worship*, Church House Publishing, 1995, p.36)

Introduction *(Show everyone the Easter candle)* When you came into church this morning you may have noticed that this candle was laid down on a table, unlit, to symbolize Jesus lying in the tomb. We will now lift it up and light it to show Jesus rose again on Easter Day. And we say, 'Christ is risen!'

All **He is risen indeed. Alleluia!**

Reading John 20.1-18

Talk I am going to ask some children to help me make four journeys to and from the Easter garden.

First we need a Mary Magdalene. She finds the tomb empty and *stays there* feeling *very sad*. Then we need two disciples. They *run to the tomb* because they hear that something strange has happened. When they get there *they stop, looking puzzled*. They *go back* the way they came. Mary Magdalene stayed at the tomb and saw Jesus alive. She *ran* from the tomb *excited and happy*.

Song 'Thank you Lord for Easter Day'. (Adapted from 'Thank you Lord for this fine day' JP 232.) *(During this song, turn the footsteps around to make two tracks leading from the Easter garden, down the aisle towards the back)*

Talk I now need two more volunteers to come and stand, not by the garden, but on the tracks leading away. Not all of Jesus' friends heard the good news that he had risen. Two of them were very sad, and felt that there was no point remaining in Jerusalem. So they decided to *walk* home to their village of Emmaus. As they walked, a stranger came alongside them *(act the stranger yourself)* and they talked. They *stopped* at their home and invited the stranger to stay. As he said grace at supper and broke the bread (*mime*), they realized they had seen Jesus. They *ran back* to Jerusalem, full of happiness and excitement.

Song 'Give me oil in my lamp' (JP 50). (*During the song, remove some foot-prints from one set of tracks down the aisle, so there are some obvious gaps.*)

Talk We have been thinking about the way friends of Jesus followed different tracks that first Easter weekend. But what about us? There is a very familiar story that you see printed on cards and calendars. Let's re-tell it now. (*Walk down the aisle as you tell the story.*)

Once upon a time a man had a dream. He was walking along the seashore, thinking about his life. He noticed two sets of footprints in the sand, representing his life. He realized that one set was his and the other footprints belonged to Jesus. He remembered all the good things that had happened to him, but also the sad times as well. Then he noticed that at the very times the sad things had happened, there was only one track in the sand. (*Stop by a gap in the tracks.*) The man felt upset about this so he prayed, 'Lord, why was it that at the very times I needed you most you weren't there?' Then he heard the voice of Jesus answer, 'My child, I have never left you. Those times when you can see only one set of steps, I was carrying you.'

This is the wonderful news of Easter Day. Jesus promises us: 'I am with you always.'

Confession Oh Jesus Christ, risen master and triumphant Lord,
we come to you in sorrow for our sins,
and confess to you our weakness and unbelief.

We have lived by our own strength,
and not by the power of your resurrection.
In your mercy, forgive us.
Lord, hear us and help us.

We have lived by the light of our own eyes,
as faithless and not believing.
In your mercy forgive us.
Lord, hear us and help us.

We have lived for this world alone,
and doubted our home in heaven.
In your mercy, forgive us.
Lord, hear us and help us.

(Michael Perry, *Church Family Worship*, Hodder & Stoughton, 1986, no. 244)

Absolution   May almighty God,
who sent his Son into the world to save sinners,
bring us his pardon and peace, now and for ever. **Amen.**

Song   'He walked where I walk' (SF 172).

Renewal of baptism promises   We know that Jesus is alive and with us. So, like his friends on that first Easter Day, we can turn to him and know him and know his love. There is an old tradition that on Easter Day we do this by renewing our baptism vows – that is, saying for ourselves the promises that were said for us at our baptism, and which some of us have said again when we were confirmed.

Leader   Do you turn to Christ?

Answer   **I turn to Christ.**

Leader   Do you repent of your sins?

Answer   **I repent of my sins.**

Leader   Do you renounce evil?

Answer   **I renounce evil.**

Leader   Do you believe and trust in God the Father,
who made the world?

Answer   **I believe and trust in him.**

Leader   Do you believe and trust in his Son Jesus Christ,
who redeemed mankind?

Answer   **I believe and trust in him.**

Leader   Do you believe and trust in his Holy Spirit,
who gives life to the people of God?

Answer   **I believe and trust in him**.

Leader   This is the faith of the Church.

All   **This is our faith. We believe and trust in one God,
Father, Son and Holy Spirit.**

(*The Alternative Service Book 1980*, pp. 230, 232)

Prayers and intercessions
Offertory song   'Alleluia, alleluia, give thanks to the risen Lord' (JP 3).
The Lord's Prayer
Recessional hymn 'Thine be the glory' (HAMNS 428).

The theme of footprints can be continued in the following all-age service. Here is a suggestion for a talk for a service with uniformed organizations present.

In advance

1. Prepare a tray with seven objects: bread roll, light bulb, toy gate, toy woolly sheep, obituary column, grapes, map.

2. Hide around the church seven envelopes, each containing an 'I am' saying of Jesus written on a small OHP slide: 'I am the bread of life', 'I am the light of the world', 'I am the door of the sheep', 'I am the good shepherd', 'I am the resurrection and the life', 'I am the vine', 'I am the way, the truth and the life'.

3. Have ready: an orienteering compass, a map and OHP of that map, and a flask of water.

4. Lay paper footprints round the church, starting at the font, some going first to the lectern, some first to the altar.

Leader	Play 'Kim's game' with the tray. Show all the objects for a few seconds, then hide them from sight. As people remember the objects, write them on an OHP slide. Then get younger ones to find the seven envelopes. Put the slides at random on the OHP. Then get the children to help you match the words and objects with sayings.
Reading	John 14.1–11
Song	'The price is paid' (SF 540).
Leader	I've got some things that the Scouts and Guides especially will recognize: a compass, map and flask of water. Could someone show me how to use the compass and map? (*Get a scout or guide to do it on the OHP*). And of course, if you use this compass and map and go on a long walk, you'll get thirsty, and be glad of a drink of water from this flask. If we think of what Jesus said, we can compare the compass to the way, the map to the truth and the water to the life.
Song	'I am the Way, the Truth and the Life' (JP 89).
Leader	There are footprints laid round the church just as we did at Easter, but today they are starting at the font, some going first to the lectern, some to the altar. I'd like some children to come and follow the trails with me. The trail starts at the font, where most of us started our Christian journey, where we were baptized. Jesus has been the **way** for us ever since. The trail is leading to the lectern, where we keep the Bible, which tells us the **truth** about Jesus. Last of all we follow the trail to the altar, where we go for holy communion or for a blessing, reminding us that Jesus gives us new **life**.

(*This talk can lead easily into the creed or a more all-age affirmation of faith.*)

© John Muir

The Resurrection

This is a simple sketch that could easily be performed by a group of five children.

Cast

Jesus
Mary Magdalene
Mary Cleophas
Angel
Peter

(Mary Magdalene and Mary Cleophas arrive at the tomb.)

Mary M   Cleophas, I'm so sad about the master. The only thing we can do is make him ready for his funeral.

Mary C   This jar of ointment is heavy. It's not much further to the tomb. Look, Magdalene, the stone that sealed the entrance has been rolled away.

Mary M   What's that? The light is so bright, it hurts my eyes.

Mary C   It's probably because you've been crying so much.

Mary M	No, it's that young man – his clothes are shining. Cleophas, I'm scared – I can't see Jesus' body anywhere.
Angel	Don't be frightened. I know you're looking for Jesus, who was crucified. He isn't here. Don't you remember? He said he'd rise on the third day.
Mary M	How can we be sure?
Angel	You must believe, and go and tell John and Peter and all his disciples that they'll meet him in Galilee.
Mary M	You go, Cleophas. I don't know what to think.
	(*Cleophas goes to tell John and Peter. Magdalene starts to cry.*)
Angel	Why are you weeping?
Mary M	Because someone has taken Jesus away and I don't know where they have put him.
	(*She sees Jesus standing outside the tomb.*)
Mary M	Are you the gardener?
Jesus	Woman, why are you crying? Who are you looking for?
Mary M	Sir, if you've moved him, tell me where he is, and I'll take him away.
Jesus	Mary . . .
Mary M	(*Kneeling*) Master.
Jesus	Don't touch me. It isn't time yet for me to go to my Father. Tell my friends that I will be going to our God and Father soon, but they will see me before that.
Mary M	Yes, Master (*She gets up.*)
Peter	What's all this? Mary Cleophas has been telling us such stories.
Mary M	It's the master, risen from the dead.
Peter	Jesus – can you forgive me for saying I didn't know you?
Jesus	Peace be to you. As the Father has sent me, so I send you. I give you the gift of the Holy Spirit. If you forgive anyone's sins, they are forgiven. Go and teach everyone in the whole world what I have taught you.

© Sheila Ward Ling

Pentecost

All ages celebrate Pentecost

A special procession in which children take part can be an enrichment of the Eucharist service at Pentecost. It can become even more significant if it is preceded by a session of work on the previous Sunday, or by an all-age workshop on the Saturday of the Pentecost weekend. Both the procession, and a special way of handling the intercessions, can be prepared at this time.

Workshop ideas

1.   The first aim of the workshop is to encourage those taking part to make simple banners in either material or coloured paper. Eventually, these are either to

be fastened to poles and carried, or to be hung from window-sills or galleries – just as people in medieval times used to welcome a king by hanging up rich carpets and lengths of fabric.

First, though, ideas for design will need to be generated. So, start by talking about the story of Pentecost and how we recognize the presence and gifts of the Holy Spirit. What are those gifts? Let those taking part give the ideas. In what situations have they been seen, or are they needed, today? Think about affairs in the Holy Land, Northern Ireland, Bosnia, Africa, and also about our own local area, our church, our lives.

Then people can decide which aspect of the work or person of the Spirit they want to portray, and they can choose relevant symbols. The traditional images can, of course, be used – the dove, the fire, the wind – but see if they can devise new symbols for the gifts which they will have talked about. Encourage people to relate their symbols of gifts – like love, strength, peace – to the events in the world and the local community that they mentioned. Do not suggest that words should be added to the banners. Words often limit people's freedom of imagination and thought, both when they make, and when they look at, banners. Symbols should be able to stand alone.

Decorate your church with the hangings and carry the banners in a procession of all ages to begin and to end your service.

2.   In the same workshop session, as preparation for the intercessions, encourage everyone to draw – or have some ready drawn to be cut out – a figure of a man or woman. Let each person choose a 'saint' who has shown the work of the Holy Spirit in his or her life. They might choose a well-known saint like Peter or another apostle, Paul, Francis, Clare, or Teresa of Avila. They may prefer to think of a local saint or great Church figure, or even those whom they would consider saints today. Ask everyone to colour and name their cut-out figure. Make sure that the backs of the figures are left blank.

Before the Sunday service, give the figures to people as they enter your church. If possible, you should have enough for one each. If not, give one per family or couple. Have pencils available. Just before the intercessions, the priest or worship leader can invite everyone to write a word or a short sentence on the back of their figure. This can be about some hap-pening or area of life in which they are grateful for the presence and strength of the

Holy Spirit, or some area in which they may need his help. The intercessions then include a time of silence to offer these thanks or requests to God. The figures are collected by children with trays or baskets at the offertory, and taken up to the altar in the offertory procession. (After the service they should be taken to the vestry and disposed of carefully.)

Ideas for a sermon or talk at Pentecost

The Holy Spirit is the unexpected person of the Trinity – unpredictable and often unwelcome. He stirs us to actions that we would often rather not take. He rouses us to be sorry, or to stretch out in forgiveness, to serve, to carry on when strength seems gone, to hope when everything seems impossible, to trust when our faith in God and in other people seems dead. The promised fruits of the Spirit – love, joy, peace, kindness, gentleness, trustfulness, goodness and self-control – are fruits of the *lifelong* presence of the Spirit. They are not sudden gifts. The suddenness is often our recognition of his presence, which overwhelms us. We then have to *work hard* in his strength to bring forth the fruits, which are the proof of his activities, and are shown in their richness in the lives and work of saints through all the ages – and of all ages today.

The blessing and dismissal

The blessing   The Spirit of truth lead you into all truth, give you grace to confess that Jesus Christ is Lord, and to proclaim the word and work of God: and the blessing . . .

The dismissal

Priest   Go forth into the world, rejoicing in the power of the Spirit.

People   **Thanks be to God.**

Some suggested hymns

'When God of old came down from heaven' (EH 158).
'Spirit of mercy, truth and love' (EH 631).
'O Holy Spirit, Lord of Grace' (HAMR 231).
'Our blest Redeemer' (HAMR 230).
'Come, Holy Ghost, our souls inspire'(EH 153).
'Be still for the presence of the Lord' (SF 40).
'Spirit of the living God (SF 510).

© Bernard Ramsay

Wine or Spirit?

This conversational sketch requires only two actors and can be performed without any props.

One   Where on earth have you been? I've been sent out to look for you! If we don't hurry back the meal will be ruined!

Two   I've been in the square with the others.

One   What, with that crowd of drunks who were shouting and waving their arms about this morning?

Two   They weren't drunk. They were . . . inspired.

One   They sounded drunk to me, and what they were shouting about I don't know. I couldn't make out half of it.

Two   That was the amazing thing that got so many people listening. Maybe some people could only understand part of what they were saying. But everyone seemed to understand *some* of it, wherever they came from.

One   You must be joking! There are people from all over the place in Jerusalem at the moment. How could they understand?

Two   Don't ask me – I'm just an ignorant local! I just stopped to see what the fuss was all about.

One   Just raving drunks. You want to watch who you mix with.

Two   They weren't drunk, I tell you. They were inspired, bubbling over with excitement and happiness. You *had* to stop and listen.

One   I didn't have to stop or listen, I just came home. Who were they anyway?

Two   They're the followers of that young teacher Jesus.

One   Oh my life! The people you get involved with. He was executed weeks ago – a common criminal.

Two   But *they* say he was God's Son, the Messiah, and it was *our* fault he was executed. And I believe they're right.

One   You can't be serious! He's dead and buried, and so's the movement he started.

Two   But that's not true. He rose from the dead, and it's his spirit that inspired those people this morning.

One   I've never heard such nonsense! I reckon there's more wine than spirit in those fellows. And what's this . . . you're wet through.

Two   I'm so sure they're right, I've joined them – I've been baptized.

One   What have you done? Why couldn't you have just come home like me?

Two   I'm just sorry for you that you didn't stay. But I did and I wouldn't have missed it for anything.

One   Just come home and forget it all.

Two   Now it's you who must be joking. It's the most important thing that's ever happened to me.

One   What – joining a dozen noisy drunks on a Sunday morning?

Two   No, being filled with a new spirit with hundreds of other folk who feel the same.

One   In a couple of days it will all be forgotten, you mark my words. Things will quieten down again and everything will be back to normal.

Two   That's just where you're wrong. Nothing will ever be the same. This is the start of something that will go on and on – you'll see!

© John Cooper

Pentecost crafts

A flame screen

Materials

plain paper
tissue paper
templates of flame
shapes
gold or silver paper
or sweet papers
a large piece of
background paper
or wallpaper
glue (a glue stick
works well)
powder or poster
paints
spray varnish

1. Paint plain paper yellow, orange and red, and allow to dry.

2. Cut it, and the tissue and gold or silver paper, into fairly large flame shapes using a template. (*It is easy to cut several flames at a time by putting layers of paper together.*)

3. Glue the bottom edge of each of the flames and stick them to a large square of background paper, with a good mixture of haphazard colours.

4. Overlap the flames and bend them a little forward so they look lively.

5. Pin up the collage on a wall and, if possible, have a leader spray it with varnish.

Flame mobile (for five to seven-year-olds)

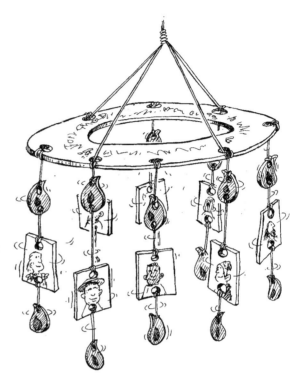

Materials
coloured card (*red, yellow, orange*)
pair of compasses
felt-tip pens
scissors
alphabet templates to write
'*Tongues of Fire*'
magazines and newspapers to cut
out pictures of people's faces

1. Draw two circles on card with your compasses and cut out the resulting ring. Write '*Tongues of Fire*' around it.

2. Colour in the letters with felt-tip pens.

3. Cut out the circle and punch eight holes at regular intervals for the hanging thread and the mobiles.

4. Draw 16 flame shapes on the coloured card, and colour the reverse of the card if it is plain.

5. Cut them out and punch a hole at the top and bottom of eight flames, and one just at the top of the others.

6. Cut out pictures of people's faces from all over the world and put them on the squares.

7. Thread the flames and the pictures to each other and to the circle, making sure the mobile is balanced.

8. Hang the mobile up by four threads that interweave.

Zig-zag books (for eight-year-olds and over)

Materials

2 sheets plain A4 paper for each child

scissors

sticky tape

pencils, paints, felt-tip pens or crayons

1. Fold the longest side of each sheet of paper in two and cut very carefully along the folds.

2. Sellotape the strips of paper together, making sure they are placed edge to edge. You should now have a very long strip of paper.

3. Fold one end to the other, then fold again and then twice more. The long strip is now small and bulky.

4. Press the folded paper under a heavy book for ten minutes to sharpen the creases.

5. The folds you have made will bend either way, so after pressing, crease the sixteen folds alternately backwards and forwards to make a zig-zag book.

6. The first and last two folds are for covers. You are left with twelve sections in which to draw a different apostle.

7. To indicate the amazing way the apostles spoke in different languages, choose twelve ways of saying, 'Praise God!' and write one for each apostle. You can make the words come out of their mouths, or write them underneath.

8. You could try to make the background to the apostle fit the culture of the language in which he is speaking.

9. Decorate the front and back covers of your book.

© Susan Holliday

Ups and downs

A group mime for four people, who respond to the narration, following the stage directions. Older children could perform this very effectively.

The Christian life is full of ups and downs,

(*The group look happy, smiling for a photograph*)

Highs and lows,

(*Suddenly look miserable*)

Peaks and troughs,

(*Laugh together*)

Thrills and spills.

(*Cry on each other's shoulders*)

Like Goliath threatening to eat the Israelites for lunch,

(*One of the group becomes Goliath, others look terrified*)

Only to meet a small boy who gave him a cracking headache before breakfast.

(*All watch Goliath tumble*)

Or Peter walking on water,

(*One of the group balances, the others watch*)

Only to sink manfully beneath the waves while his friends watched.

(*Others hide smiles as one sinks*)

Following Jesus has often been like that. First there were the miracles,

(*One person becomes blind and is healed by another*)

Closely followed by the complaints from the Church.

(*Other two grab them*)

Then there were the amazing stories,

(*One talks, others listen*)

Followed by the lies from the religious leaders.

(*Others gag him, placing their hands over his mouth*)

Next came the parties and meals,

(*Eat, talk, drink, laugh*)

Followed by torture and death.

(*The group pretends to crucify one of them, back to audience*)

And most surprising of all, the return from the dead.

(*Lean on each other looking depressed. Then look off-stage, amazed*)

Then the return to heaven,

(*Look up, mouths gradually dropping open*)

And Jesus' friends found themselves alone.

(*Back up against the wall*)

Abandoned with nothing.

(*Huddle together*)

Nothing except the ultimate power of the Holy Spirit.

(*Suddenly drop to the floor*)

And so the Christian Church was born. With a few frightened people and the power of God.

Nothing changes much, does it?

(*Freeze in positions of praying for one another.*)

© Dave Hopwood

Blow, blow, wind of God

A poem exploring some of the symbols of the Holy Spirit.

Blow, blow, wind of God
    Gale of anger,
    Breeze of blessing.
Blow, blow, wind of God
Breathe on us your power.

Burn, burn, flame of God
    Fire of purging,
    Blaze of glory.
Burn, burn, flame of God
Warm us with your fire.

Rest, rest, bird of God,
    Dove of peace,
    Wings of shelter.
Rest, rest, bird of God,
Sing to us of home.

Flow, flow, stream of God,
    Spring of life,
    River of healing.
Flow, flow, stream of God,
Revive us with your grace.

Drop, drop, rain of God,
    Showers of love
    Tears of gladness.
Drop, drop, rain of God,
Slake our thirsting hearts.

© Don Dowling

Harvest

Harvest

An all-age service

> *'He who supplies seed to the sower and bread for food, will supply and multiply your sowing and increase your righteousness'* *(2 Corinthians 9.10).*

Our harvest of praise

Use the following hymns and songs to begin the service on a note of praise:
'Thank you Lord for this fine day' (SF 524; JP 232).
'From the rising of the sun' (*plus actions*) (SF 121; JP 49).
'Great is thy faithfulness' (*especially verse 2 and the chorus*) (SF 147; JP 64).

A collect for harvest

Almighty and everlasting God, we offer you our heartfelt thanks for your goodness and care in giving us the fruits of the earth in their seasons. Give us grace to use them rightly to your glory and for the good of others and the relief of those in need, through Jesus Christ our Lord, Amen.

The harvest of forgiveness – a time to say sorry

After each bidding of the prayer, the people respond: **Forgive us, Lord.** *Different members of the congregation could lead at this point. Make sure all age groups are represented, if possible.*

Lord, we are sorry that in each of us there is a part of that greed that has meant that many starve while we go well fed.

Forgive us, Lord.

Lord, we are sorry that we have taken for granted the good things we have so readily to hand and forgotten our neighbours who have to go without.

Forgive us, Lord.

Lord, we are sorry that we have not done our part in sharing the goodness you have so freely shared with us and that we have kept hold of things as if they were our own by right rather than gifts from you.

Forgive us, Lord.

Lord, we are sorry that our lives have too often been marked by selfishness rather than gratefulness.

Forgive us, Lord.

Lord, we are truly sorry and repent of all our sins.

Forgive us, Lord.

The words of absolution could perhaps include the following words from Isaiah 44.21-22:

'I formed you; you are my servant; you will not be forgotten by me. I have swept away your transgressions like a cloud and your sins like a mist. Return to me for I have redeemed you.'

A harvest psalm of thanksgiving

Psalm 67. This psalm lends itself to being read as a dialogue. After each section said by the leader, the congregation replies:

May the peoples praise you, O God; may all the peoples praise you!

A harvest of sharing

This is the time to bring up harvest gifts and also to share church family news together — including birthdays, thanksgivings and prayer requests. At this point in the service, one of the children's groups could contribute either a song or a piece of drama, as another way of sharing gifts with the congregation.

To end this time, sing a hymn like:

'For the beauty of the earth' (JP 48; SF 112).

Some special harvest prayers

Use some of the harvest prayers from Mary Batchelor, *Lion Book of Children's Prayers*, Lion Publishing 1994, or from Michael Botting, *Prayers for all the Family*, Kingsway, 1993.

Finish by saying the *Lord's Prayer* together.

The harvest of the word

Use three different people to read the following short passages on the theme of harvest:

John 12.24

James 5.7–8

Luke 18.1,7–8

The harvest of prayer: a story for harvest

Use the pictures and words on an overhead projector.

Transparency 1 Just in case anyone was still in doubt, let me remind you that '*It's harvest!*' But, for many people, there is a perfectly natural follow-up question: '*So what?*'

Not many people today get to see the work in the fields – the actual harvest. Most of us are city people. What's so special about harvest, when we can go to the shops and get what we want at any time of the year? Why make a fuss of harvest? We should be thankful all year round, shouldn't we?

I think God has some particular things to teach us through harvest, some important gospel truths. To tell you about them, I need to introduce you to a friend – someone who would really like to be up there on the table with the gifts!

For this, you need to use a 'cuddly' toy mouse which, with a bit of simple practice you can animate. You could get the mouse to run up your arm, then try and escape, and maybe meet some of the children.

This is Harvey, the harvest mouse. Now, Harvey has a tale to tell. A story of the meaning of harvest. To do this he wants to introduce us to three of his friends.

Transparency 2   There's Woody, the wood mouse, Furry, the field mouse, Dozy, the dormouse, and here's Harvey again – he's quite proud of this portrait.

It all started almost a year ago. They all lived by a lovely wild field near . . . (*name a local spot*). The field was a sort of playground for them all, a beautiful place with plenty of cover and wild blackberries. But one day disaster struck. The field was bought by a human and things began to change. The four friends watched carefully and wondered.

First, the ground was cleared and dug over by a machine. It was terrible. The field was no longer beautiful. There were no blackberries to eat. Nowhere to play hide and seek. Just a muddy, black desert. Young Woody cried: 'What a mess!' *Transparency 3* 'There's no point staying here anymore – I'm off back to the woods.'

Some time later there was more activity in the field. Another machine came, scattering little yellowy bits everywhere which then got churned over into the soil and buried out of sight. Furry, who was watching, got quite agitated. 'All those bits of food being thrown away – just being buried and lost for ever,' she said. 'What a waste! I'm not staying around here anymore in this graveyard.' And with that, she too was off into the wood and gone for good.

Months passed. Young Dozy kept a lazy eye on the field. He hoped that things would somehow get back to the way they were, but nothing happened. Just the rain and the sunshine, the frost and the cold, day in, day out. Dozy kept hoping but in the end he too decided to give up. It wasn't worth waiting anymore. 'What a long wait!' he sighed. 'It's obvious that the field will never come back to the way it was. I'm off somewhere new like the others.' He yawned his goodbyes and left. Only Harvey stayed and watched and waited.

Slowly, things did begin to happen. Little green bits appeared above the surface of the soil. They grew and grew, taller and thicker, gradually taking over every square centimetre of the field – and slowly but surely turning it all a golden yellow in the sunshine. A field full of corn, rich corn, a paradise for Harvey. Better than it had been before, full of food and places to hide and to play. 'What a miracle!' he squeaked. The miracle of the harvest that comes to the one who didn't give up waiting.

Do you see what Harvey learned? One of the messages of harvest from God to us all.

First of all, a harvest takes *patience*. In our instant world, where we want everything by yesterday, we need to learn that the best gifts, God's gifts, take time. His ways aren't often instant. God will answer our prayers and work out his plan for us, even though things may have to be messy and even wasteful for a while.

A harvest teaches us about *prayer*. Prayer is about staying on the look-out, like Harvey – keeping our eyes on what God is doing, staying close to him, even when nothing seems to be happening. God is always at work and if we listen carefully and watch closely, he will share the secret of what he is doing with us. Prayer is staying alert, like Jesus asked of the disciples in Gethsemane, in spite of the many temptations to give up.

Finally, a harvest teaches us to follow his *pattern*, the pattern of Jesus. The only way to a harvest of good news is to go the Jesus way, the way of dying, or being trampled down and buried. Only then can we rise again to a new and glorious resurrection life. Jesus taught this and did it. He died for us in our place. He can help us to go the same way and produce a harvest for him.

'It's harvest, so what?' God has some special things to teach us through harvest. Maybe we should change the question slightly.

Transparency 4   'It's harvest, sow what?'

Sow *patience*, sow *prayer*, and sow a life *patterned* on Jesus.

Follow Harvey's example and learn this lesson of harvest and discover the miracle of Jesus at work in your lives this coming year.

Final (offertory) harvest hymn

'We plough the fields and scatter' (JP 267; SF 585).

The blessing

The final prayer might include the following verse: 'Let us not grow tired, for at the right time we shall reap a harvest, if we do not lose heart' (Galatians 6.9).

Instructions for transparencies

Transparencies number 1 and 4 just have writing on them.

No. 1 says in big letters: 'It's harvest!

So what?'

No. 4 says the same thing with the same placing of letters, with just one difference:

'It's harvest!

Sow what?'

The illustrations for transparencies number 2 and 3 are shown overleaf. These can be enlarged on a photocopier and then photocopied or traced on to an acetate sheet.

© Martyn Payne

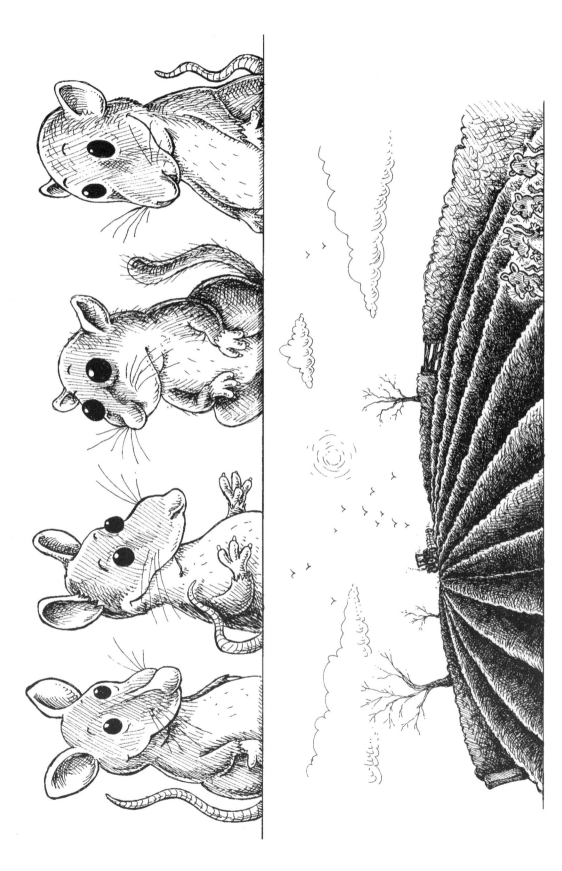

Activities for harvest

At harvest time, we want children to have the opportunity to express thanksgiving to God for the multitude of material gifts we enjoy in this part of the world. At the same time, we want them to be growing in their awareness and concern for those parts of the world where people only know poverty, famine and drought. These harvest-time craft activities are designed to help children to hold these two expressions together.

With the under-fives

Draw a large outline of a very full supermarket trolley on strong backing paper or card. Have an ample supply of empty cartons, wrappers, labels, plastic bottles and so on. Make pretend food tins by sticking wrappers around cardboard tubes. Help the children to rummage among the containers and find their favourite foods. As you do this, talk about the wide range of flavours, colours and textures of food there are. Then stick the containers onto the outline drawing of the supermarket trolley.

Cut out large letters to spell THANK YOU. Invite children to draw their favourite food – or stick small pictures of food – on to the letters. This THANK YOU caption can be displayed near the overflowing shopping trolley picture in church or in the room where the children meet. Children can use this display as the visual focus for their harvest-time thank-you prayers:

Thank you, Lord, for harvest time, and for all that you provide for us. Thank you for . . . (*Here, the children mention the items which they have chosen for the large trolley.*)

'Help us to share the things that we have with others. Help us not to be greedy and selfish, taking more than our share. Help us always to remember that you are the giver of all good gifts and to say thank you for them. Amen.

With the five- to nine-year-olds

Fold a sheet of thin A4 card or stiff paper in half.

Make a template of a very full supermarket trolley that fits this size of paper. Place the template onto the card with the handle of the trolley to the folded edge. Cut out the shape of the shopping in the trolley so that the card is shaped like the shopping trolley. Be sure to leave the folded edge intact, so that the card opens.

Invite the children to write their own prayers or provide prayers already typed onto little pieces of paper that will fit the card. Open up the supermarket trolley card and on one side of the card, write or stick a THANK YOU prayer for our harvest time. On the facing page, put a PLEASE prayer for those suffering from the effects of famine and drought.

Encourage the children to take away their prayer cards to use at home as well.

With the over-tens

Get two large pieces of hessian or other suitable material for a banner or wall hanging. Encourage the group to talk about their favourite foods. Ensure that you have enough variety between their choices – you may have to encourage the inclusion of certain things to get this variety. Cut pieces of fabric to the size and shape of dinner plates and invite the young people to use any kind of material to make a collage of their favourite meal on their plate.

This range of meals can then be arranged complete with fabric cutlery on the first banner with the simple caption THANK YOU. Be sure that the banner is full. This is part of the visual impact of the abundance of the gifts we receive.

On the second banner, put one empty or almost empty fabric bowl or plate with the caption PLEASE.

While working on this, be prepared to discuss the problems of poverty in the world, and ways of sharing more generously. Maybe even plan some form of activity that the group can do to express their concern.

Display the banners in church for the harvest thanksgiving service. They will provide a stark reminder of the reality of the world situation and a meaningful focus for prayer during the service. If possible, arrange for the young people themselves to write, and then read out, short prayers, based on the two banner themes.

© Betty Pedley

115

Harvest gifts

A simple sketch about the way we can give our lives to God. It is particularly appropriate at Harvest or Christmas but can also be used with the 'St Francis — a life given to God' on pages 113 – 118.

The two children, Dave and Simon, should be played by adults. They are scruffy, chewing gum, pulling their clothes, scratching, etc. While they talk, they mess about with their school ties (if they have them) and saunter around the stage. The dialogue is written for two boys, but with a few changes it would suit two girls.

The two enter together.

Dave   'Ere, my mum said that we've got to go to church on Sunday.

Simon   (*With a big smile*) I know.

Dave   My mum said that we've got to go because it's Harvest Sunday (*or Christmas, Easter or another festival*).

Simon   I know.

Dave   My mum said that we've got to take something to give to God to say 'Thank you'.

Simon	I know.
Dave	Well . . . what you gonna take then?
Simon	(*Pause. With a cheeky grin*) Guess.
Dave	I dunno . . . a sprout?
Simon	Nope.
Dave	A bag of carrots?
Simon	Nope.
Dave	(*Hopefully*) Not that conker you beat me with last week?
Simon	Don't be stupid! Course not.
Dave	I know – your Batman T-shirt?
Simon	(*Looks inside his jumper*) Nope.
Dave	Not your BMX bike?
Simon	Something much better than all of that.
Dave	But there isn't anything better than that.
Simon	Oh yes there is.
Dave	Oh no there isn't!
	(*Repeat this, involving the audience.*)
Dave	What then?
Simon	(*Another pause*) Me!
Dave	But you can't give yourself to God on Harvest Sunday!
Simon	Oh yes I can.
Dave	Oh no you can't.
	(*Repeat again.*)
Dave	All right then – how?
Simon	Easy. Easy-peasy-lemon-squeezy! I'll tell you. (*Takes a deep breath*) I'm gonna ask God if I can be his best friend – and I'm gonna let him be mine!
Dave	You mean – your bestest, bestest friend?
Simon	Yep – my bestest-bestest-everest friend!
Dave	Wow!
	(*Both freeze.*)

© Dave Hopwood

Blackberries

This story explores the ways that children can enjoy God's creation in the most unlikely of settings.

Behind the house, at the end of the garden, was some waste ground. Nobody bothered with it. Some people threw junk onto it. It was of little use to anyone. Brambles grew all over it, sometimes covering the junk.

Tom and Daisy did not play on the waste ground. It was not that their mother would have stopped them, it was that there was nothing on the waste ground that was any use to play with. They had the garden. If they wanted a bigger space they had the park. There were many things to do and many things to play with. The waste ground was useless. It was close to the railway line, so it was noisy. Tom and Daisy ignored it.

One day, in early autumn, their mum said, 'Do you want to come to help me pick some blackberries?'

'Yes, please,' said the children although they were not sure what blackberries were or how you picked them.

To their surprise, Mum took them to the end of the street, where the railway line ran, and down a small path that went round the back of the row of houses, which formed their street. They found themselves on the waste ground.

'Now you must be careful here,' said Mum, 'People leave their rubbish here. Watch where you put your feet.'

They walked carefully across the ground towards a huge mound of brambles. Mum stopped in front of the bushes and produced some pots from the bag that she was carrying.

'Now you see the berries?' She pointed to them. The children nodded. The berries were big black and shiny. 'Only pick the ones that look like this. Don't pick fruit that is still red. Those berries are not ripe yet. Don't pick fruit that is all shrivelled up, just pick big juicy berries. Oh, and watch out for the prickles. I would like us to fill all these pots so that we can have some to eat now and some to put in the freezer.'

She picked two large ripe berries and popped one into Tom's mouth and one into Daisy's mouth. The fruit was sweet and juicy. Both children grinned.

After that Mum picked busily. Tom picked some fruit and a few berries even found their way into the pot he was holding, but he ate most of the berries that he picked. Daisy was not sure about those prickles so she picked carefully and very slowly. Even so she still managed to get a prickle in her finger.

When Mum had picked as much fruit as she wanted she stopped the children. She wiped Tom's mouth where the juice had trickled down his chin and she found the prickle in Daisy's finger and got it out.

'Come on now, let's go home,' she said.

As she turned she saw a sharp face in the undergrowth. It was red. It had bright eyes and sharp teeth. It looked like a small dog. Tom and Daisy saw it too. It was a fox. The fox looked at them for a moment, with its head slightly to one side, and then it turned and disappeared into the bush and down towards the railway embankment.

'Well, I thought that there must be a fox living near here, but I didn't think that I would see it that close,' said Mum.

'Why does it live here?' asked Daisy.

'I think that it feels safe here. Hardly anyone comes onto this piece of ground and it can always run down onto the railway embankment. There are probably lots of small animals living here for it to eat.'

'Oh,' said Daisy, not sure if she liked the idea of a fox eating other animals.

'Let's go home,' said Mum. 'I need to put these berries in the freezer.'

'Don't we have to pay for them?' asked Tom.

'No, dear, they are free.'

'But you always have to pay for fruit in the shops.'

'Yes, that's because the farmers have to grow them and pick them and the shops have to sell them. Blackberries grow naturally and we have picked them so we don't have to pay for them.'

'Do other people know about blackberries?'

'Yes, I expect so, dear.'

'Why don't they pick them too?'

'I don't know, dear. Perhaps they don't think that it's worth the effort.'

Daisy had popped a large, shiny blackberry into her mouth. 'I like blackberries,' she said. 'I think that they are worth picking, even if I did get prickled.'

After the blackberry picking, the children would often look out of the back window of their house trying to see the fox again, but they never did. They still do not go onto the waste ground on their own. There was nothing there to play with and they did not want to disturb the fox.

Of course, they did go back again next year with their mum to pick blackberries.

All Saints/Saints

Light and laughter

There are many ways of providing an enjoyable and fun alternative party to Hallowe'en for children. The following ideas give some practical suggestions on how to plan and run such a party.

We decided several years ago to start offering an alternative to Hallowe'en activites. We realized children need clear messages to equip them to cope with the darker side of life, but definitely wanted them to continue having fun. We also recognized our duty to welcome non-church children whose parents might be unaware of the potential harm lurking behind the fun of Hallowe'en. Since then, our 'light and laughter' party has become established as a popular event attended by over one hundred children, fulfilling the original aim of providing good, clean fun on 31 October.

Our progress has not been without difficulties and we have learnt a great deal along the way, but perhaps these tips will help others.

121

Prayer

An obvious need, but easily forgotten in the frantic activity associated with most children's work. We always pray at planning meetings and during a brief moment of calm just before we open the doors and let the hordes in. We also ask our congregation to support us in prayer.

Publicity

We have found the following ideas helpful:

* Fun invitations and posters for church children, and those linked with church.

* Posters in schools and library displaying a brief explanation as to why we are providing an alternative event.

* Involving the whole church through an article in the church magazine.

* Inviting the local press to an advance publicity photo session. One year our party was the only one featured.

We always stress that places must be booked in advance so that we can plan properly.

Date and time

We have concluded that the event *must* be held on 31 October, even if inconvenient for adults, and start fairly late in the day. Both of these factors ensure that the aim of the event, providing a genuine alternative, is met, and children do not have the chance for other possible activities. Any clashes with uniformed organizations has usually been overcome by inviting them to join forces.

Christian message

The 'light and laughter' parties always attempt to be great fun. But we do also get the Christian message across, with a short service at the beginning where we stress that God wants us to celebrate all that is good in the world. This is followed up in activities, songs and informal discussion. The theme of light, of course, lends itself to many exciting activities, and seems very appropriate when days are getting dark. We have used various Bible passages including John 8.12, Luke 8.16 and Mark 4.21. We have also sometimes focused on saints.

Activities and organization

Because we now have so many children coming, we usually divide into age-groups for everything except our opening service. On arrival, every child is checked in and given a name label. The label's colour indicates which group to go in. We suggest a £1 donation per child as parents seem to prefer having an idea of how much to give.

We quickly learned to offer a constant stream of activities to prevent children inventing their own. The children move from one activity area to the next in rotation at intervals of 10 to 15 minutes. As well as the essential team games and musical games to work off energy, here are some things we have found to be successful:

Saints and symbols   Explain briefly a few saints' stories. Then send children to find hidden cards depicting their symbols, like St Peter's rock, St Patrick's shamrock and so on.

Blindfold games   Once blindfolded, get children to draw a self-portrait, trust someone to take them for a walk, and so on.

Torch games   In a separate darkened room, each child sits on the floor with a torch. Play 'musical torches', with torches flashing around the room until the music stops or 'follow the leader', where the leader's coloured light has to be chased, and shine torches to form the cross of Christ on the ceiling.

Cake or biscuit icing   Very popular, and sticky.

Candle crafts   Wax-resist painting, decorating household candles, making rolled candles from honeycomb wax, available from candle-craft shops or beekeepers.

Collage candles   Stick down card or paper shapes for candle and holder. Add string wick and foil or a Cellophane flame.

Model candles   Use a covered or painted toilet roll for the candle, a round cheese box holder and foil or Cellophane flame.

Mounted prayers   Use holders that come with school or other photographs and insert hand-written or photocopied prayers. Illustrate or decorate.

Grand finale

We end with sparklers outside followed by a rousing sing-song before the children go home laden with their crafts, candles, cakes and a friendly letter telling parents about our church groups. This outreach has really borne fruit, and many of our families have found a way into church via children's parties and activities. Children's events may be exhausting, but there is a great deal of fellowship and satisfaction to be found in providing local parents and children with a real welcome on a night when they could be drawn further away from God's family.

© Gail Silver

Celebrating the saints of God
An all-age service

Welcome

Opening sentence   Luke 7.47

Leader   Let us come into God's presence.

Holy Spirit help us pray,

All   **Give to God the praise and glory,**

Leader   Fill us all with power today,

All   **Give to God the praise and glory,**

Leader   Though we cannot see, we know,

All   **Give to God the praise and glory,**

Leader   You are here like years ago,

All   **Give to God the praise and glory,**

Leader   Give us voices full of praise,

All   **Give to God the praise and glory,**

Leader   Pleasing God in many ways,

All   **Give to God the praise and glory.**

(From Peter Graystone and Eileen Turner,
A Church for All Ages, Scripture Union, 1993, p. 115.)

Hymn   'To God be the glory' (JP 259).

Saints and symbols quiz (maximum 10 minutes)

For this you need to have the older children's groups doing some preparation in the week before the service. They need to look up saints in a book and draw the symbols that go with the saints on sheets of A3 paper. Then they paint the symbols. On the back of each sheet is written the name of the relevant saint, plus two other saints' names.

In the service itself, divide the congregation into two teams. The younger children hold up the symbols one by one for each team to guess in turn which saint it belongs to. If no one can guess, turn the sheet round to give them the three clues. Once they have guessed correctly, individual children explain why that symbol was used for that particular saint.

You can do the scoring on an acetate. For every correct answer give a letter, gradually spelling SAINT for one team and ALIVE for the other. The first team to complete a word wins.

Symbols and saints

St Catherine	Catherine wheel
St Martin	Soldier's helmet / cloak torn in half
St Luke	Stethoscope / bag
St Francis	Birds and animals
St Charles the Martyr	A guillotine and long wavy hair
St Julian of Norwich	A heart with 'All shall be well'
St Oswald	A crown and a plate of food
St Peter	A rock with a church on top
St Alban	Drops of blood turning to roses
St Boniface	An axe and a tree trunk
St Margaret	A crown next to an oyster shell with a pearl
St Patrick	A shamrock clover leaf
St Stephen	A pile of stones
St Paul	A kneeling figure and bright light
St Andrew	A white X-shaped cross on a blue background

Talk   Go on to say that although the church has canonised some people, which means they are especially remembered as being faithful to God, at this time of year we remember *all* the saints. We can't know all their names, but God does, just like he knows us.

Hymn   'I sing a song of the saints' (JP 115).

Reading   Luke 7.36–50 (*The woman who washed Jesus' feet with her tears*)

This reading can be done very effectively in four sections. For each section, ask the congregation to close their eyes and listen, while someone reads very clearly. In the meantime, children at the front pose in relevant positions as if for a photograph. After each section, invite the congregation to open their eyes and spend a moment looking at the scene and thinking about the feelings of the biblical characters.

Read   Verse 36

Scene   Pharisees and Jesus reclining at table. (*Pause.*)

Read   Verses 37–38

Scene	Woman and Jesus, Pharisees looking on. (*Pause.*)
Read	Verses 39–53
Scene	Jesus explaining to Simon, woman and other Pharisees looking on. (*Pause.*)
Read	Verses 44–50
Scene	Woman being raised up by Jesus and forgiven. (*Pause.*)
Songs	'Jesus' love is very wonderful' (JP 139).
	'Whether you're one' (JP 284).

Talk

The visual aid for this talk needs careful advance preparation. Open a conventional tin of dog food at the bottom. A wall can-opener gives a very clean cut. Empty the tin and wash and dry both tin and lid very thoroughly, ensuring the label remains glued on.

Make a new filling for the tin. Make up a packet of chocolate mousse like Angel Delight. Before it sets, cut up a Mars Bar into thin slices and melt a little in a saucepan or microwave. Stir gently into the mousse and pour into the upside down tin, ensuring the Mars Bar chunks go in first. Fill the tin to the top. Put on the lid and secure it with very discreet glue or tape. Put the tin in the freezer. For best results, you need to use it 45 minutes after taking it from the freezer.

You will also need a tin opener, a clear bowl, some spoons and kitchen roll to lay them on. It looks very effective and tastes delicious!

Aim

* If we judge people from the outside we often get it wrong.
* Jesus said it's what we are like inside that counts.
* Saints are people changed on the inside by God's love.

Open the tin explaining you have started a new high-protein diet someone has told you about. Put some food in the bowl. (*It is important not to react to the congregation's horrified response.*) Carry on talking about its good qualities and eating the 'dog food' that you have put into the bowl. Go down into the congregation, letting them see close up, and ask for some volunteers to try some. One or two brave souls might volunteer. Once they have said how nice it tastes, every child will want to join in. Tell them they can at the end of the service.

Then make the link between people's responses to you eating 'dog food' and the Pharisees' horrified response to Jesus and the woman in the reading. The people who become saints are often the most unlikely ones who do not perhaps look special, but are changed inside to be new people who love God and others. Saints are not just the famous ones we remember like Francis, but all the thousands of ordinary people who have loved Jesus. They know they have been forgiven much, therefore they love much. We often think we can know about people by their expressions and their clothes. But God looks inside, and so should we. If we are to be saints, we have to look closer and give people a chance, just like those who tried the dog food, and discovered it was a chocolate mixture. (*At this point tell children not to eat real dog food at home.*)

When God changes us, it is real, not a trick. As we pray today, let us ask God if he will change us inside to be people who love much, people who know Jesus died for us to be forgiven much.

Hymn   'Father we love you' (JP 45).

Prayer of confession

Leader   Holy God, parent of us all, we know we don't always treat each other as you want us to. Lord God, forgive us,

All   And help us to be more loving.

Leader   There are times when we insist on getting our own way, despite what others feel. Lord God forgive us,

All   And help us to be more loving.

Leader   Sometimes we increase the tension when we ought to be seeking to make peace. Lord God, forgive us,

All   And help us to be more loving.

Leader   Often we say things which hurt each other. Lord God, forgive us,

All   And help us to be more loving.

Leader   For our jealousy, our lack of respect, and times when we won't listen to those we live with, Lord God, forgive us,

All   And help us to be more loving.

Leader   And because we sometimes just get bored with each other,

Lord God, forgive us,

All   And help us to be more loving.

The Lord's Prayer

Final hymn   'O when the saints go marching in' (JP 195).

© Jacqui Hill

St Francis – a life given to God

An all-age service

The life of St Francis is remembered each year on 4 October. His fascination with God's creation, his challenging lifestyle and his care of others provide plenty of inspiring ideas for all-age worship.

As everyone comes in to church, give them a piece of paper and a pencil, and ask them to put them under their seats until they are needed.

Song   'O give thanks to the Lord' (SF 413).

Prayers of thanksgiving   *These help to set the scene for the theme of the service. The thanksgiving prayers from* Church Family Worship, *no. 478, work well at this point.*

Introduction   The theme for today's service is our response to God. What can we give him, and how can we respond to him in thanks for all he has given to us?

Telling the stories

Start by looking at two rich young men. Both of them had been given a lot of material wealth, but their responses to their riches were very different.

1.   Reading   Matthew 19.16–22 The story of the rich young man that Jesus met.

This story can either be read straight, or with different people reading the words of Jesus and the young man. Or, if you prefer, embellish the story a little and ask some children to come and act it out.

2.   St Francis

Tell the story of the first part of Francis' life, using adults to mime it. This can be done with minimal rehearsal.

Francis was born over 800 years ago, about 1182, in Assisi in Italy. He was named John by his mother, but his father changed his name to Francis. His father was a cloth merchant, and Francis went into the same trade. He was a very sociable and generous young man and he loved going out singing and playing sports with friends of his own age. His family was very wealthy and Francis enjoyed having money to spend on himself, though he was also very generous in giving to those in need.

When he was 20, Francis was taken prisoner during a battle in Assisi and was in captivity for a year. Shortly after this he was seriously ill for some time and it was during this illness that he decided to devote himself to prayer and service of the poor. He went on a pilgrimage to Rome, changed clothes with a beggar and spent the rest of the day begging. This made him very aware of the whole issue of poverty and when he returned to Assisi he spent his time caring for lepers and helping rebuild a ruined church. He said to his father that he wanted nothing more to do with him or all his wealth and possessions. The story even says that he stripped naked on the steps of the bishop's palace and his father walked off with his clothes.

From then on, Francis wore a long dark garment tied with a cord, and lived a life of poverty, begging for his food and owning nothing himself.

So, here are two very different rich young men. The first was unwilling to give up all his wealth, whereas the second, Francis, gave up all his riches and possessions to live a life of poverty.

Song   'Thank you Jesus' (SF 523).

St Francis and the animals

Continue the story of St Francis, this time without mime.

Francis is probably best remembered as the saint who loved animals, and he was always full of praise and thanks for the wonder of God's creation. There are various stories about Francis and how he tamed different animals. For example, one story tells of a city that kept being attacked by a fierce wolf who ate not only animals but people, and everyone in the city was terrified. Francis went out to meet the wolf, although everyone told him not to. When the wolf saw Francis, he came running towards him growling, but Francis commanded him in the name of God the Father to lie down, and the wolf immediately did so. Francis was able to lead him tamely into the city.

Francis was truly grateful to God for all he gives us in creation.

At this point, ask some children to come and hold up posters of beautiful scenes, flowers, and animals.

Towards the end of his life, Francis wrote a hymn of praise to God, calling on everything and everyone in the world to give praise and thanks to the Father. The hymn we are going to sing now is based on the one written by Francis.

Hymn   'Great is thy faithfulness' (SF 147).

St Francis and the friars

Conclude the story of St Francis.

The way of life that Francis had chosen attracted other men who wanted to do the same. They followed his example, and eventually they all became established as the order of Friars Minor. Their one rule of life was that of complete poverty, they could not own any possessions or accept any money. A similar order was set up for women by St Clare, a lady from Assisi. The friars cared for those suffering from leprosy and preached the gospel. In everything he did, Francis always wanted to be poor, because he did not want any worldly possessions or worries to come between him and God.

Song   'Make me a channel of your peace' (SF 381).

Remind everyone that this is the prayer of St Francis set to music.

Sketch   'Harvest gifts' by Dave Hopwood (see pages 122–124).

Introduce the sketch by reviewing what has been said so far, reminding everyone about the contrast between the rich young man in the Gospel of Matthew, who was willing to give up nothing, and Francis, who was willing to give up everything. Then ask about us. What does God want us to give to him? What is the most important way for us to respond to him?

Song   'In my life Lord, be glorified' (SF 242).

Drawing and talking

Ask the children to draw on their pieces of paper some pictures of things that God has given us in his creation, like mountains and rivers, flowers, animals, seas, people, trees and so on.

While they are doing this, talk briefly to the adults, something like this:

Giving of ourselves and our possessions to God is a strong theme in the Bible. Listen to some of the verses about it in the New Testament.

Luke 6.38
Matthew 6.1–4
2 Corinthians 9.6–7
Luke 21.1–4

These verses show:

1.   What our *attitude* should be towards giving.

2.   *How* God wants us to give.

3.   *What* we should give to God. For example, ourselves, our time, and our money.

Our aim must be similar to Francis, to put God absolutely first in everything we do, whatever implications that will have for our lives. For all of us, there will be areas of our lives that we need to give more fully to God. Maybe it is our giving of money, or maybe something quite different, like our use of time, our relationships, our leisure interests or our praying.

Then ask the adults to think about one area of their lives they want to give over more fully to God. Suggest that they write it down on their bit of paper. Warn them that you will use a few of them for a prayer of dedication near the end of the service.

Song   'Father, we love you' (SF 102).

During this song, the children come and stick their pictures on a board and a box is passed round the adults for them to put their bits of paper in.

Prayers

•   *Use the pictures the children have drawn as a basis for a simple prayer of thanksgiving for God's creation.*

•   *Give thanks for the life of St Francis, praying for courage for us to be as wholehearted in our devotion to God as he was.*

•   *Use some of the suggestions the adults have written down, and pray a prayer of dedication to God.*

Offertory hymn   'Take my life and let it be' (SF 519).

Offertory prayer

Suggested prayer, Church Family Worship (no. 460), Hodder & Stoughton, 1986.

The blessing

> Lord, make us instruments of your peace.
> Where there is hatred, let us sow love;
> where there is injury, let there be pardon;
> where there is discord, union;
> where there is doubt, faith;
> where there is despair, hope;
> where there is darkness, light;
> where there is sadness, joy;
> for your mercy and for your truth's sake. Amen.

© Sue and Hamish Bruce

St Barnabas the bold

11 June is the feast of St Barnabas. His contribution to the life and witness of the early Church is often overshadowed by the fact that we know so much more about St Paul. But to look at his life and work is to be challenged to greater faith and faithfulness. It is not a story that is easily accessible to children, but maybe the activities here will help.

The following story can be read straight out, and then the activities can be done afterwards. Or, the story can be broken up where the star marks are, and the activity, discussion and prayer for that section can be done before proceeding. The ideas are most relevant to seven-year-olds upwards, though they could be simplified for younger ones.

Materials for the activities

For each section: candle and matches.

Activity 1	Ready-made plain badges, or circles of card, safety pins and tape. Colourful pens and gummed shiny stars.
Activity 2	Magazine pictures of assorted food. Scissors and glue. Maybe a picture of a child with a bowl of rice from one of the aid agency publications.
Activity 3	Writing paper – maybe with envelopes to ensure privacy.
Activity 4	Large piece of paper and marker pens.
Activity 5	Pens and paper.

Final activity: pens, card and scissors.

The story

St Barnabas is one of the saints from the New Testament. He came from the island of Cyprus, but the first time the Bible mentions him is when he is in the city called Jerusalem which was the place where the very first group of Christians began. One of the first things the Bible says about him is that *Barnabas* was his nickname. His real name was Joseph, but the leaders of the church in Jerusalem started calling him Barnabas. The name means 'son of encouragement'. He was always seeing how to help other Christians. (Activity 1)

One of the ways he did that was to be generous with his money. When he saw that some of the poorer believers needed money, he sold a field that he owned and gave the money to the church leaders to help the poorer Christians. (Activity 2)

Another time, Barnabas helped a man called Saul. It happened like this: in the time when Barnabas lived, there were people who hated Christians and tried to kill them. Saul was one of the men most determined to get rid of all the Christians. He was always travelling to different places to find if there were Christians there so that he could make trouble for them.

One day, though, all that changed. Saul had a vision of Jesus. It was like a very clear dream, though Saul was not asleep. As a result, Saul decided he had to become a follower of Jesus too. After a while, he went to Jerusalem to meet the leaders of the church. But they would not believe that he was really a changed man. They did not even want to talk with him. They thought he was trying to trick them.

Only one person was brave enough to find out if Saul was telling the truth. That was Barnabas. He brought Saul to the church leaders and helped them to understand that Saul really had changed. (Activity 3)

After that, the leaders of the church in Jerusalem realized even more what a good man Barnabas was. So when they wanted to find out about a new group of Christians in another city called Antioch, they decided to send Barnabas to check it all out. They were worried because they were not sure that the new believers were real Christians. So Barnabas went to Antioch and was really excited to discover these new Christians. He decided to stay to help them — and he went to get his friend Saul to come to help them too. (Activity 4)

After a year in Antioch, the people of the church there were praying one day, and the Holy Spirit told them to pray especially for Barnabas and Saul, as there was special work for them to do.

This was a new beginning for Barnabas. The rest of the Bible's report about him tells of his travels, first with Saul, and then with another man called Mark. They went from city to city to tell people about Jesus. They had many adventures, and sometimes life was very dangerous for them. But all the time, Barnabas knew that more than anything he wanted to pass on the good news about Jesus.

We are not told about the end of Barnabas' life. But we do know that in Cyprus today, people still honour him as the one who first brought the message of Jesus to that island. (Activity 5)

Activity 1   Nicknames

If you have read the Mr Men story books, you will see that Barnabas was a bit like Mr Happy — always trying to help other people. In fact, if he were here today, his nickname might be Mr Encourager. Think about your family or your friends. Is there someone who is especially good at being kind, or helpful, or full of fun, or cheerful?

Maybe you could be an encourager like Barnabas by making them a Mr Men badge. On a circle of card write the name — something like Mrs Helpful, Miss Jolly, or Mr Friendly — in special letters. Then decorate it with shiny stars, and stick a safety pin on the back with tape.

Then keep it to give them at a quiet moment.

Prayer   Light a candle and thank God for each of those people who are going to be given a badge.

Activity 2   Being generous

Barnabas was very generous to poor people. Are there ways in which children can help poor people? How about the Blue Peter appeals? Or Comic Relief?

Make a simple collage with a large number of pictures of food that we enjoy in this country on one half – and a simple bowl of rice on the other.

Prayer   Light a candle and pray for all the people who are poor and in need.

Activity 3   Bold and brave

Barnabas was very brave to trust Saul, the man who had tried so hard to kill Christians. Sometimes God calls us to do things that seem scary or too difficult for us. Sometimes there are things in our life that make us very afraid.

Write a private letter to God, telling him the things that make you afraid and asking for his help. No one else is to see your letter. You can tear it up or keep it safely after the session.

Prayer   Light a candle and pray for courage every time you are afraid.

Activity 4   Looking for good

When Barnabas went to Antioch, he did not just start looking for what the new Christians might be doing wrong. He was really excited to meet them.

People in this country are often good at moaning. We moan about the weather, the prices in shops, the government, the vicar . . . on and on and on. Maybe we can be more like Barnabas, and look for the good.

On a huge piece of paper, write: 'Thank you God for . . .' in the middle. Then have a brainstorm session and write or draw all the things that are brilliant about living in your town, village or area.

Prayer   Light a candle and, with your eyes open, thank God for all the things on the sheet.

Activity 5   Ready and willing

Barnabas was ready and willing to do new things and go to new places for God. Some Bibles have maps in them to show just where he and Saul went. Have a look at one of those maps.

Draw a map of the place where you live, marking on it all the places you go each week, like: home, school, clubs, shops, church, friends' houses, and so on.

Prayer   Light a candle and pray that God will go with you wherever you go.

Final activity

Make a bookmark and draw a picture of what you think St Barnabas looked like. Write on it: 'I like St Barnabas because . . .' and fill in your own answer.

Prayer   Light a candle and thank God for St Barnabas.

© Pam Macnaughton

St Thomas

The life and legends of St Thomas provide both challenge and inspiration. Here are a number of activity suggestions to explore the possibilities for the feast day on 3 July.

Thomas the faithful doubter

The fourth Gospel has three pictures of St Thomas.

1.   John 11.16. Thomas shows that he will be faithful to Jesus.

2.   John 14.5. Thomas shows that he is not frightened to ask questions when he does not understand.

3.   John 20.24–31. Thomas needs to discover the truth of the resurrection for himself. He won't believe because others tell him to. He needs to say, 'I can't believe this unless . . .'

Activities

These could be adapted to include all ages.

The three pictures of Thomas could be explored by doing some of these activities.

•   Create a 'faithfulness' poster.
This could include:
names of people I trust
those who trust me
pictures-signs-symbols
Bible verses (use a concordance).

•   Questions box or questions time.

Invite people to contribute questions in response to: 'Everything I wanted to ask about . . .'

Either write them down – or divide into pairs to talk them through.

Don't put one person into the role of having to give answers. Use it as an opportunity for as many people to respond as possible.

•   Set up a 'graffiti doubting board'

Invite people to respond to: 'I can't possibly believe this . . .'

Adults' comments alongside children and young people's may spark off some interesting comments and discussions.

Most important: the aim is to listen, *not* to make people believe 'six impossible things before breakfast' (as in the story *Alice in Wonderland*).

The activity is about giving space and permission for people to voice important thoughts.

Thank God for doubting Thomas.

Thank God for questions.

Thank God for these signposts on the faith journey.

Thomas the traveller

According to tradition, Thomas was the apostle who travelled from Jerusalem through Persia – now Iran – to India. The Christians of the Kerala district in India have called themselves 'St Thomas Christians' for centuries.

Activities

•   Trace the route Thomas took on a map. How many different countries do you pass through?

•   Today there are many Indian Christians. Christian Aid and Traidcraft have many projects in India. Organize a Traidcraft or Christian Aid exhibition showing their Indian projects. Contact your local or area representatives for help. Organize a Traidcraft stall and sell Indian produce.

Thomas the builder

Another tradition says that whilst in India, Thomas built a church with his own hands. Thomas is sometimes called the patron saint of builders and architects.

Activities

•   Remember and pray for all architects, builders, bricklayers, carpenters, roofers, plasterers and decorators. Are there any of these who could come and talk about their work?

•   Design a St Thomas thank-you card. Say thank you for all that builders do in your community. Deliver the card – and say why.

•   If Thomas built a church today, what would it look like? Create you own designs, models etc. If possible, invite builders or architects to give advice or comment.

Story: Thomas and the golden palace

A legend says that one of the rulers in India had heard that Thomas was a skilled architect and builder. He asked Thomas to build a beautiful palace, and gave large quantities of gold and silver to complete the work. After giving his orders, the ruler then left on a long journey.

Not long afterwards, there was a serious famine in the area and Thomas used the silver and gold to buy food for the starving people.

On his return, the ruler was furious and threw Thomas into prison and ordered his execution.

The ruler's brother fell seriously ill. In a dangerous fever, he had a dream of a beautiful palace built in heaven.

'Thomas has built it for you,' he groaned to the ruler. 'It will be yours after death if you prove worthy.'

The brother recovered from the fever, and Thomas was set free. The legend ends with the ruler and his brother being baptized by Thomas.

Activities

• Dramatize the story.

• Paint or draw your vision of the heavenly palace. What would make it heavenly for you?

• Create some brick shapes from coloured card or paper. Invite people to write a concern or need on the brick shape. Gather them together to make a wall or building. You could charge people for their card shape and then send the money to Christian Aid or some other charity.

• Create St Thomas shields.

1. First, paint a red background.

2. Then paint a carpenter's square with a silver blade and gold handle.

3. Finally draw a spear with a silver head and brown handle.

(See *Saints, Signs, Symbols*, SPCK, p. 15.)

Believe and be bold

Richard Jenkins wrote this hymn for the patronal festival at his church. The final verse will not be relevant to all, but the last line of the third verse provides a strong alternative ending

Tune   Hanover

1.   We gather today to learn and receive
     From one who said firmly: 'I will not believe,
     Until to my touch is presented the mark
     Of nail and of sword, and of deeds in the dark!'

2.   Into our Lord's side he stretched forth his hand.
     'Believe from now on, in trust take your stand.'
     So healing flowed forth from the marks of the sword,
     And Thomas then witnessed: 'My God and my Lord!'

3.   Like Thomas we strive to trust in that night,
     When faith has grown cold and comfort is slight.
     Then Jesus invites us, as Thomas of old:
     'Reach forth now and touch me – believe and be bold.'

4.   And so now we offer on St Thomas' Day,
     With Malabar Indians on coasts far away,
     Our praise and thanksgiving and joy without end,
     To Thomas our patron and faithful soul-friend.

© Peter Privett

Bad – and good – King Wenceslaus

The following article tells the story behind the famous carol and clears up some confusion between the two Kings Wenceslaus.

There were two kings called Wenceslaus, but only one of them was good. Let's look at him first, the one we sing about at Christmas.

Wenceslaus was a very young king. He was murdered by his twin brother, Boleslaus, when he was only 22 years old. They were born in 907. Their father was a Christian, but their mother, Drahomira, was not. The boys were only eight years old when their father died. By that time Wenceslaus was already a duke and had gone to live with Ludmilla, his saintly grandmother. Boleslaus stayed with his mother. So Wenceslaus was brought up as a Christian and Boleslaus as a pagan.

People could see the difference. The story soon buzzed around about when young Wenceslaus left his castle one freezing night to take care of a poor old man. They saw that he would be a just, merciful ruler – and Boleslaus quite the opposite.

You know the way rival football teams have their support clubs? Well, the Christians and pagans supported the two boys like that, only more so. Drahomira hated Ludmilla and hired assassins to murder her. The pagans strangled the old lady with her own veil as she knelt and prayed. Wenceslaus appealed to the emperor for protection. The emperor made him king, and gave support to him and all the Christians in the country. There was a great battle, Christians against pagans. Wenceslaus was the victor, in spite of being badly wounded.

Wenceslaus was still a loving, obedient son. His mother asked to see him so he went, although he knew how wicked she was. On his way he popped into a church to pray, unaware that Boleslaus was waiting in ambush. His brother murdered him, then chopped his body in pieces. Three years later Boleslaus realized how wicked he had been, and confessed his sins. When he became a Christian, the whole country followed his example. Pilgrims still visit Prague cathedral to see the shrine where the remains of St Wenceslaus were laid to rest. His grandmother became a saint too, St Ludmilla.

And now for the bad King Wenceslaus, born about 400 years later. There had been two more King Wenceslauses during that time, so this one was King Wenceslaus the Fourth. He was a lazy drunkard, and treated his wife cruelly. But the queen had a friend, a priest called John. John was the son of a poor farmer, born in the village of Nepomuk. The boy was too frail to help his father, so they sent him to study to become a priest.

John helped the queen to take care of the poor people, and taught her the Christian faith. Like many Christians, the queen would confess her sins to John, and he would tell her of God's forgiveness.

King Wenceslaus became jealous. Whatever could the sins be that the queen confessed to John? He roared at John: 'I demand to know what the queen has told you!' John refused. In a drunken rage, the king had the priest imprisoned and tortured, but still the good man wouldn't tell. Although the queen pleaded for him, Wenceslaus hated John more and more. At last, he had John bound hand and foot and thrown into the river. The body sank. Then, as the king watched, it bobbed up again. A halo of five stars hovered over the water. The king went mad, jumped on his horse, and rode off, and stayed away for a long time. But John's body was buried and he became St John of Nepomuk. Pictures of him always show the halo of five stars around his head and his finger to his mouth. He was the saint who wouldn't tell a secret.

Why not make a badge or bookmark of St Nepomuk, to remind you to be good at keeping secrets?

© Margaret Spivey

The story of St Nicholas

6 December is the feast of St Nicholas. Use the story below to tell small children one of the legends about him. Older children will enjoy the cartoon version by Simon Smith. It could be photocopied as part of an Advent worksheet.

Hundreds of years ago there lived a good and holy bishop in the Church at a place called Myra. His name was Nicholas and he often wore a long red cloak and bishop's hat. He was quite rich, but he did not spend his money on himself. Instead, he liked to help the poor, especially children, and to give them presents without being seen.

One day, Nicholas heard about a father who had three daughters. He so wanted them to get married, but he was too poor to pay for their weddings. He was very, very sad, and wondered who would look after them when he was old.

Nicholas opened his large chest of money and took out a bag of gold. When it was dark he hurried out to the poor man's house, and finding an open window, he threw in the bag of gold, and no one saw him. When the father, who had been sitting with his head in his hands, heard a noise, he looked up and found the money. He was delighted. Now he could pay for a wedding for one of his daughters. However, there were still the other two daughters. The next night the man sat crying, wondering what to do. Suddenly, another bag of gold dropped into his open window. The man jumped up to see who had brought it, but he was too late. He picked up the money with a grateful heart. Now he could afford a wedding for his second daughter.

There was still one more girl, the youngest daughter. The father began to wonder if his unknown friend, who always came after dark, knew that he had three girls. He decided to hide outside his window just in case the kind person came again. He did not have to wait long before he heard soft footsteps hurrying towards his house. Then a hand reached out from under a cloak, and a bag was thrown through the window. This time, the poor father caught hold of the stranger's cloak. To his great surprise, he saw that it was the good Bishop Nicholas. He was full of gratitude as he knelt to thank the bishop who quickly disappeared into the night.

© Phyllis A. Jackson

Together
with Children

*I*f you have found the material in this book useful, why not subscribe to the parent magazine? *Together with Children* provides practical, topical resource material, information about wider issues in Christian children's work, and inspiration for leaders. Every issue contains:

- A COMPLETE ALL-AGE SERVICE
- ONE OR MORE STORIES
- SKETCHES FOR CHILDREN TO PERFORM OR WATCH
- AN ARTICLE ABOUT AN ISSUE IN CHILDREN'S WORK
- A REPORT OF GOOD WORK BEING DONE
- BOOK REVIEWS

There are also activity ideas for a saint's day or festival, readers' letters and an opinion column.

FREE sample copies are available from the National Society at the address below.

ANNUAL SUBSCRIPTIONS (9 issues per year: monthly during school term), are available from The National Society, Church House, Great Smith Street, London SW1P 3NZ.

DISCOUNTS are available for multiple-copy subscriptions going to the same address (e.g. for two leaders working together, or for one of the clergy as well as the children's leader). For more details contact: The National Society, Church House, Great Smith Street, London, SW1P 3NZ. Telephone: 0171 222 1672; Fax: 0171 233 2592; e-mail: ns@natsoc.demon.co.uk.